THE ENGLISH IN INDIA

THE ENGLISH IN INDIA

REPRINTED FROM COLONIZATION AND CHRISTIANITY

WILLIAM HOWITT

GYAN

Published by

Gyan Publishing House
5, Ansari Road
Daryaganj, New Delhi-110002
Phone: 011-47034999, 9811692060
E-mail: books@gyanbooks.com

Distribution Network
gyanbooks.com
India, USA, Canada, UK, Australia

ISBN: 978-93-7097-259-9 (PB)

First Published, 1839

2nd Impression 2026

Printed at: Gyan Press, Delhi.

THE ENGLISH IN INDIA
Author: WILLIAM HOWITT

THE

ENGLISH IN INDIA;

REPRINTED FROM

"COLONIZATION AND CHRISTIANITY:"

A POPULAR HISTORY OF THE TREATMENT OF THE NATIVES BY THE EUROPEANS IN ALL THEIR COLONIES.

BY WILLIAM HOWITT.

"Most of the countries in India have been filled with tyrants who prefer piracy to commerce—who acknowledge no right but that of power; and think that whatever is practicable is just."—*The Abbe Ray*

Second Edition.

WITH AN APPENDIX.

LONDON:

LONGMAN, ORME, BROWN, GREEN, AND LONGMANS.

1839.

The following Chapters are (by the kind permission of Messrs. LONGMAN & Co., *and with the very cordial approbation of the esteemed Author) extracted from the valuable work of* Mr. HOWITT, *entitled* "COLONIZATION AND CHRISTIANITY," *and reprinted in their present form in the hope that they may be more extensively read, and create a feeling in behalf of the Country to which they refer, that may soon receive a practical and beneficial application.*

CONTENTS.

THE ENGLISH IN INDIA.

CHAPTER I.

SYSTEM OF TERRITORIAL ACQUISITION.

"And Ahab came into his house, heavy and displeased, because of the word which Naboth the Jezreelite had spoken to him; for he had said, I will not give thee the inheritance of my fathers. And he laid him down upon his bed, and turned away his face, and would eat no bread. But Jezebel his wife came to him, and said unto him, Why is thy spirit so sad that thou eatest no bread? And he said unto her, Because I spoke unto Naboth the Jezreelite, and said unto him, give me thy vineyard for money; or else, if it please thee, I will give thee *another* vineyard for it; and he answered I will not give thee my vineyard.

And Jezebel, his wife, said unto him, Dost thou now govern the kingdom of Israel? Arise, and eat bread, and let thine heart be merry; I will give thee the vineyard of Naboth the Jezreelite.

* * * * * * *

And the word of the Lord came to Elijah the Tishbite, saying, Arise, go down to meet Ahab king of Israel, which is in Samaria; behold he is in the vineyard of Naboth, whither he is gone down to possess it. And thou shalt speak unto him saying, Thus saith the Lord, Hast thou killed, and also taken possession?" 1 *Kings* xxi. 4-19.

THE appearance of the Europeans in India, if the inhabitants could have had the Bible put into their hands, and been told that that was the law which these strangers professed to follow, must have been a curious spectacle. They who professed to believe the commands that they should not steal, covet their neighbour's goods, kill, or injure—must have been seen with wonder to be the most covetous, murderous, and tyrannical of men. But if the natives could have read the declaration of Christ —"By this shall men know that ye are my disciples, that ye love one another,"—the wonder must have been tenfold; for never did men exhibit such an intensity of hatred, jealousy, and vengeance towards each other. Portuguese, Dutch, French, English, and Danes, coming together, or one after the other, fell on each others forts, factories, and ships with the most vindictive fury. They attacked each other at sea or at land; they propagated the most infamous characters of each other wherever they came, in order to supersede each other in the good graces of the people who had valuable trading stations, or were in possession of gold or pearls, nutmegs or cinnamon, coffee or cotton cloth. They loved one another to that degree that they were ready to join the natives anywhere in the most murderous attempts to massacre and drive away each other.

What must have seemed most extraordinary of all, was the English expelling with rigour those of their own countrymen who ventured there without the sanction of the particular trading company which claimed a monopoly of Indian commerce. The rancour and pertinacity with which Englishmen attacked and expelled Englishmen, was even more violent than that which they shewed to foreigners.

The history of European intriguers, especially of the Dutch, Portuguese, English, and French, in the East, in which every species of cruelty and bad faith have been exhibited, is one of the most melancholy and humiliating nature. Those of the English and French did not cease till the very last peace. At every outbreak of war between these nations in Europe, the forts and factories and islands which had been again and again seized upon, and again and again restored by treaties of peace in India, became immediately the scene of fresh aggressions, bickerings, and enormities. The hate which burnt in Europe was felt hotly, even to that distance; and men of another climate, who had no real interest in the question, and to whom Europe was but the name of a distant region which had for generations sent out swarms of powerful oppressors, were called upon to spill their blood and waste their resources in these strange deeds of their tyrants. It is to be hoped that the bulk of this evil is now past. In the peninsula of India, to which I am intending in the following chapters to confine my attention, the French now retain only the factories of Chandernagore, Caricall, Mahee, and Pondicherry; the Portuguese—Goa, Damaun, and Diu; the Dutch—Serampore and Tranquebar; while the English power had triumphed over the bulk of the continent—over the vast regions of Bengal, Madras, Bombay, the Deccan and the Carnatic—over a surface of upwards of 500,000 square miles, and a population of nearly a hundred millions of people! These states are either directly and avowedly in British possession, or are as entirely so under the name of allies. We may well, therefore, leave the history of the squabbles and contests of the European Christians with each other for this enormous power, disgraceful as that history is to the name of Christianity—to inquire how we, whose ascendency has so wonderfully prevailed there, have gained this dominion, and how we have used it.

When Europe sought your subject-realms to gain,
And stretched her giant sceptre o'er the main,
Taught her proud barks the winding way to shape,
And braved the stormy spirit of the Cape;
Children of Brama! then was Mercy nigh,
To wash the stain of blood's eternal dye?
Did Peace descend to triumph and to save,
When free-born Britons crossed the Indian wave?
Ah no!—to more than Rome's ambition true,
The muse of Freedom gave it not to you!
She the bold route of Europe's guilt began,
And, in the march of nations, led the van!—*Pleasures of Hope.*

We are here to witness a new scene of conquest. The Indian natives were too powerful and populous to permit the Europeans to march at once into the heart of their territories, as they had done into South America, to massacre the people, or to subject them to instant slavery and death. The old inhabitants of the empire, the Hindoos, were indeed, in general, a comparatively feeble and gentle race, but there were numerous and striking exceptions; the mountaineers were, as mountaineers in other countries, of a hardy, active, and martial character. The Mahrattas, the Rohillas, the Seiks, the Rajpoots, and others, were fierce and formidable tribes. But besides this, the ruling princes of the country, whether Moguls or Hindoos, had for centuries maintained their sway by the same power by which they had gained it, that of arms. They could bring into the field immense bodies of troops, which though found eventually unable to compete with European power and discipline, were too formidable to be rashly attacked, and have cost oceans of blood and treasure finally to reduce them to subjection. Moreover, the odium which the Spaniards and Portuguese had everywhere excited by their unceremonious atrocities, may be supposed to have had their effect on the English, who are a reflecting people; and it is to be hoped also that the progress of sound policy and of Christian knowledge, however slow, may be taken into account in some degree. They went out too under different circumstances—not as mere adventurers, but as sober traders, aiming at establishing a permanent and enriching commerce with these countries; and if Christianity, if the laws of justice and of humanity were to be violated, it must be under a guise of policy and a form of law.

We shall not enter into a minute notice of the earliest proceedings of the English in India, because for upwards of a century from the formation of their first trading association, those proceedings are comparatively insignificant. During that period Bombay had been ceded as part of a marriage-portion by the Portuguese to Charles II.; factories had been established at Surat, Madras, Masulipatam, Visigapatam, Calcutta, and other places; but it was not till the different chartered companies were consolidated into one grand company in 1708, styled "The United Company of Merchants trading to the East Indies," that the English affairs in the east assumed an imposing aspect. From that period the East India Company commenced that career of steady grasping at dominion over the Indian territories, which has never been relaxed for a moment, but, while it has for ever worn the grave air of moderation, and has assumed the language of right, has gone on adding field to field, and house to house—swallowing up state after state, and prince after prince, till it has finally found itself the sovereign of this vast and splendid empire, as it would fain persuade itself and the world, by the clearest claims, and the most undoubted justice. By the laws and principles of modern policy, it may be so; but by the eternal principles of Christianity, there never was a more thorough repetition of the hankering after Naboth's vineyards, of the "slaying and taking possession" exhibited to the world. It is true that, as the panegyrists of our Indian policy contend, it may be the design of Providence that the swarming millions of Hindostan should be placed under our care, that they may enjoy the blessings of English rule, and of English knowledge: but Providence had no need that we should violate all his most righteous injunctions to enable him to bring about his designs. Providence, the Scriptures tell us, intended that Jacob should supersede Esau in the heritage of Israel: but Providence had no need of the deception which Rebecca and Jacob practised,—had no need of the mess of pottage and the kid-skins, to enable Him to effect his object. We are much too ready to run the wilful career of our own lusts and passions, and lay the charge at the door of Providence. It is true that English dominion is, or will become, far better to the Hindoos than that of the cruel and exacting Moguls; but who made us the judge and the ruler over these people? If the real object of our policy and exertions in India has been the achievement of wealth and power, as it undoubtedly has, it is pitiful and hypocritical to endeavour to clothe it with the pretence of working the will of Providence, and seeking the good of the natives. We shall soon see which objects have been most zealously and undeviatingly pursued, and by what means. If our desires have been, not to enrich and aggrandize ourselves, but to benefit the people and rescue them from the tyranny of bad rulers, heaven knows what wide realms are yet open to our benevolent exertions; what despots there are to pull down; what miserable millions to relieve from their oppressions;—and when we behold Englishmen levelling their vengeance against such tyrants, and visiting such unhappy people with their protective power, where neither gold nor precious merchandize are to be won at the same time, we may safely give the amplest credence and the profoundest admiration to their claims of disinterested philanthropy. If they present themselves as the champions of freedom, and the apostles of social amelioration, we shall soon have opportunities of asking how far they have maintained these characters.

Mr. Auber, in his "History of the British Power in India," has quoted largely from letters of the Board of Directors of the Company, passages to shew how sincerely the representatives of the East India Company at home have desired to arrest encroachment on the rights of the natives; to avoid oppressive exactions; to resist the spirit of military and political aggression. They have from year to year proclaimed their wishes for the comfort of the people; they have disclaimed all lust of territorial acquisition; have declared that they were a mercantile, rather than a political body; and have rebuked the thirst of conquest in their agents, and endeavoured to restrain the avidity of extortion in them. Seen in Mr. Auber's pages, the Directors present themselves as a body of grave and honourable merchants, full of the most admirable spirit of moderation, integrity, and benevolence; and we may give them the utmost credit for sincerity in their professions and desires. But unfortunately, we all know what human nature is. Unfortunately the power, the wealth, and the patronage brought home to them by the very violation of their own wishes and maxims were of such an overwhelming and seducing nature, that it was in vain to resist them. Nay, in such colours does the modern philosophy of conquest and diplomacy disguise the worst transactions between one state and another, that it is not for plain men very readily to penetrate to the naked enormity beneath. When all the world was applauding the success of Indian affairs,—the extension of territory, the ability of their governors, the valour of their troops; and when they felt the flattering growth of their greatness, it required qualities far higher than mere mercantile probity and good intentions, to enable them to strip away the false glitter of their official transactions, and sternly assure themselves of the unholiness of their nature. We may therefore concede to the Directors of the East India Company, and to their governors and officers in general, the very best intentions, knowing as we do, the force of influences such as we have already alluded to, and the force also of modern diplomatic and military education, by which a policy and practices of the most dismal character become gradually to be regarded not merely unexceptionable, but highly honourable. We may allow all this, and yet pronounce the mode by which the East India Company has possessed itself of Hindostan, as the most revolting and unchristian that can possibly be conceived. The most masterly policy, regarded independent of its *morale*, and a valour more than Roman, have been exhibited by our governors-generals and armies on the plains of Hindostan: but if there ever was one system more Machiavelian—more appropriative of the shew of justice where the basest injustice was attempted—more cold, cruel, haughty, and unrelenting than another,—it is the system by which the government of the different states of India has been wrested from the hands of their respective princes and collected into the grasp of the

British power. Incalculable gainers as we have been by this system, it is impossible to review it without feelings of the most poignant shame and the highest indignation. Whenever we talk to other nations of British faith and integrity, they may well point to India in derisive scorn. The system which, for more than a century, was steadily at work to strip the native princes of their dominions, and that too under the most sacred pleas of right and expediency, is a system of torture more exquisite than regal or spiritual tyranny ever before discovered; such as the world has nothing similar to shew.

Spite of the repeated instructions sent out by the Court of Directors to their servants in India, to avoid territorial acquisitions, and to cultivate only honest and honourable commerce; there is evidence that from the earliest period the desire of conquest was entertained, and was, spite of better desires, always too welcome to be abandoned. In the instructions forwarded in 1689, the Directors expounded themselves in the following words: "The increase of our revenue is the subject of our care, as much as our trade:—'tis that must maintain our force, when twenty accidents may interrupt our trade;—'tis that must make us a nation in India. Without that, we are but as a great number of interlopers, united by his Majesty's royal charter, fit only to trade where nobody of power thinks fit to prevent us; and upon this account it is that the wise Dutch, in all their general advices which we have seen, write ten paragraphs concerning their government, their civil and military policy, warfare, and the increase of their revenue, for one paragraph they write concerning trade."

Spite of all pretences to the contrary—spite of all advices and exhortations from the government at home of a more unambitious character, this was the spirit that never ceased to actuate the Company, and was so clearly felt to be it, that its highest servants, in the face of more peaceful injunctions, and in the face of the Act of Parliament strictly prohibiting territorial extension, went on perpetually to add conquest to conquest, under the shew of necessity or civil treaty; and they who offended most against the letter of the law, gratified most entirely the spirit of the Company and the nation. Who have been looked upon as so eminently the benefactors and honourers of the nation by Indian acquisition as Lord Clive, Warren Hastings, and the Marquess Wellesley? It is for the determined and successful opposition to the ostensible principles and annually reiterated advices of the Company, that that very Company has heaped wealth and distinctions upon these and other persons, and for which it has just recently voted an additional pension to the latter nobleman.

What then is this system of torture by which the possessions of the Indian princes have been wrung from them? It is this—the skilful application of the process by which cunning men create debtors, and then force them at once to submit to their most exorbitant demands. From the moment that the English felt that they had the power in India to "divide and conquer," they adopted the plan of doing it rather by plausible manœuvres than by a bold avowal of their designs, and a more honest plea of the right of conquest—the ancient doctrine of the strong, which they began to perceive was not quite so much in esteem as formerly. Had they said at once, these Mahomedan princes are arbitrary, cruel, and perfidious—we will depose them, and assume the government ourselves—we pretend to no other authority for our act than our ability to do it, and no other excuse for our conduct than our determination to redress the evils of the people: that would have been a candid behaviour. It would have been so far in accordance with the ancient doctrine of nations that little would have been thought of it; and though as Christians we could not have applauded the "doing evil that good might come of it," yet had the promised benefit to more than eighty millions of people followed, that glorious penance would have gone far in the most scrupulous mind to have justified the crime of usurpation. But the mischief has been, that while the exactions and extortions on the people have been continued, and in many cases exaggerated, the means of usurpation have been those glozing and hypocritical arts, which are more dangerous from their subtlety than naked violence, and more detestable because wearing the face, and using the language, of friendship and justice. A fatal friendship, indeed, has that of the English been to all those princes that were allured by it. It has pulled them every one from their thrones, or has left them there the contemptible puppets of a power that works its arbitrary will through them. But friendship or enmity, the result has been eventually the same to them. If they resisted alliance with the encroaching English, they were soon charged with evil intentions, fallen upon, and conquered; if they acquiesced in the proffered alliance, they soon became ensnared in those webs of diplomacy from which they never escaped, without the loss of all honour and hereditary dominion—of every thing, indeed, but the lot of prisoners where they had been kings. The first step in the English friendship with the native princes, has generally been to assist them against their neighbours with troops, or to locate troops with them to protect them from aggression. For these services such enormous recompense was stipulated for, that the unwary princes, entrapped by their fears of their native foes rather than of their pretended friends, soon found that they were utterly unable to discharge them. Dreadful exactions were made on their subjects, but in vain. Whole provinces, or the revenues of them, were soon obliged to be made over to their grasping *friends*; but they did not suffice for their demands. In order to pay them their debts or their interest, the princes were obliged to borrow large sums at an extravagant rate. These sums were eagerly advanced by the English in their private and individual capacities, and securities again taken on lands or revenues. At every step the unhappy princes became more and more embarrassed, and as the embarrassment increased, the claims of the Company became proportionably pressing. In the technical phraseology of money-lenders, "the screw was then turned," till there was no longer any enduring it. The unfortunate princes felt themselves, instead of being relieved by their artful friends, actually introduced by them into

> Regions of sorrow, doleful shades, where peace
> And rest can never dwell; hope never comes
> That comes to all; but torture without end
> Still urges.

To escape it there became no alternative but to throw themselves entirely upon the mercy of their inexorable creditors, or to break out into armed resistance. In the one case they found themselves speedily stripped of every vestige of their power—their revenues and management of their territories given over to these creditors, which still never were enough to liquidate their monstrous and growing demands; so that the next proposition was that they should entirely cede their territories, and become pensioners on their usurpers. In the other case, they were at once declared perfidious and swindling —no faith was to be kept with them,—they were assaulted by the irresistible arms of their oppressors, and inevitably destroyed or deposed.

If they sought aid from another state, that became a fortunate plea to attack that state too; and the English were not contented to chastise the state thus aiding its ancient neighbour, it was deemed quite sufficient ground to seize and subjugate it also. There was no province that was for a moment safe from this most convenient system of policy, which feared public opinion sufficiently to seek arguments to make a case before it, but resolved still to seize, by hook or by crook, all that it coveted. It did not suffice that a province merely refused an alliance, if the proper time was deemed to be arrived for its seizure--some plea of danger or suspicion was set up against it. It was called good policy not to wait for attack, but to charge it with hostile designs, though not a hostile indication was given—it was assailed with all the forces in the empire. Those princes that were once subjected to the British power or the British *friendship*, were set up or pulled down just as it suited their pleasure. If necessary, the most odious stigmas were fixed on them to get rid of them—they were declared weak, dissolute, or illegitimate. If a prince or princess was suspected of having wealth, some villanous scheme was hatched to plunder him or her of it. For more than a century this shocking system was in operation; every day growing more daring in its action, and more wide in its extent. Power both gave security and augmented audacity—for every British subject who was not belonging to the Company, and therefore interested in its operations, was rigidly excluded from the country, and none could therefore complain of the evil deeds that were there done under the sun. It is almost incredible that so abominable an influence could be for a century exercised over a great realm, by British subjects, many of whom were in all other respects worthy and most honourable men; and, what is more, that it could be sanctioned by the British parliament, and admired by the British nation. But we have yet the proofs to adduce, and unfortunately they are only too abundant and conclusive. Let us see them.

We will for the present pass the operations of Clive in the Carnatic at once to destroy the French influence there, and to set up Mahomet Ali, a creature of the English. We shall anon see the result of that: we will observe in the first place the manner of obtaining Bengal, as it became the head of the empire in India, and the centre of all future transactions.

In 1756, Suraja Dowla, the Subahdar of Bengal, demanded an officer belonging to him who, according to the custom amongst the colonists there, had taken refuge at Calcutta. The English refused to give him up. The Subahdar attacked and took the place. 146 of the English fell into the conqueror's hands, and were shut up for the night in the celebrated *Black-hole*, whence only 23 were taken out alive in the morning. It may be said in vindication of the Subahdar, that the act of immuring these unfortunate people in this horrible den was not his, but that of the guards to whom they were entrusted for the night, and who put them there as in a place of the greatest security; and it may be added, not to the credit of the English, that this very *black-hole* was the *English* prison, where they were in the habit of confining *their* prisoners. As Mr. Mills very justly asks—"What had they to do with a *black-hole?* Had no *black-hole* existed, as none ought to exist anywhere, least of all in the sultry and unwholesome climate of Bengal, those who perished in the *black-hole* of Calcutta would have experienced a different fate."

On the news of the capture of Calcutta arriving at Madras, a body of troops was dispatched under Admiral Watson and Colonel Clive, for its recovery, which was soon effected, and Hoogly, a considerable city about 23 miles further up the river, was also attacked and reduced. A treaty was now entered into with Suraja Dowla, the Subahdar, which was not of long continuance; for, lest the Subahdar, who was not at bottom friendly to the English, as he had in reality no cause, should form an alliance with the French at Chandernagore, they resolved to depose him! This bold and unwarrantable scheme of deposing a prince in his own undoubted territories, and that by mere strangers and traders on the coast, is the beginning of that extraordinary and unexampled assumption which has always marked the conduct of the English in India. Scarcely had they entered into the treaty with this Subahdar than they resolved to depose him because he would protect the French, who were also permitted to hold a factory in his territory as well as they. This audacious scheme was Clive's. Admiral

Watson, on the contrary, declared it an extraordinary thing to depose a man they had so lately made a solemn treaty with. But Clive, as he afterwards avowed, when examined before the House of Commons, declared that "they must now go further; they could not stop there. *Having established themselves by force and not by consent of the Nabob*, he would endeavour to drive them out again." This is the robber's doctrine;--having committed one outrage, a second, or a series of outrages must be committed, to prevent punishment, and secure the booty. But having once entertained the idea of pulling the Subahdar from his throne, they did not scruple to add treason and rebellion to the crime of invading the rights of the sovereign. They began by debauching his own officers. They found out one Meer Jaffier Khan, a man of known traitorous mind, who had been paymaster-general under the former Subahdar, and yet retained great power in the army. This wretch, on condition of being placed on the throne, agreed to betray his master, and seduce as many of the influential of his officers as possible. The terms of this diabolical confederacy between this base traitor and the baser *Christian English*, as they stand in the first parliamentary report on Indian affairs, and as related by Orme in his History of India (ii. 153), and by Mills (ii. 110), are very instructive.

The English had got an idea which wonderfully sharpened their desire to depose Suraja Dowla, that he had an enormous treasure. The committee (of the council of Calcutta) really believed, says Mr. Orme, the wealth of Suraja Dowla much greater than it possibly could be, even if the whole life of the late Nabob Aliverdi had not been spent in defending his dominions against the invasions of ruinous enemies; and even if Suraja Dowla had reigned many, instead of one year. They resolved, accordingly, not to be sparing in their demands; and the situation of Meer Jaffier, and the manners and customs of the country, made him ready to promise whatever they desired. In the name of compensation for losses by the capture of Calcutta, 10,000,000 rupees were promised to the English Company; 5,000,000 rupees to English inhabitants; 2,000,000 to the Indians, and 700,000 to the Armenian merchants. These sums were specified in the formal treaty. Besides this, the Committee resolved to ask 2,500,000 rupees for the squadron, and the same amount for the army. "When this was settled," says Lord Clive, "Mr. Becher (a member) suggested to the committee, that he thought that committee, who managed the great machine of government, was entitled to some consideration, as well as the army and navy." Such a proposition in such an assembly could not fail to appear eminently reasonable. It met with a suitable approbation. Mr. Becher informs us, that the sums received were 280,000 rupees by Mr. Drake the governor; 280,000 by Col. Clive, and 240,000 each by himself, Mr. Watts, and Major Kilpatrick, the inferior members of the committee. The terms obtained in favour of the Company were, that all the French factories and effects should be given up; that the French should be for ever excluded from Bengal; that the territory surrounding Calcutta to the distance of 600 yards beyond the Mahratta ditch, and all the land lying south of Calcutta as far as Culpee, should be granted them on Zemindary tenure, the Company paying the rent in the same manner as the other Zemindars.

Thus did these Englishmen bargain with a traitor to betray his prince and country,—the traitor, for the bribe of being himself made prince, not merely sell his master, but give 2,398,000*l.* sterling (Orme says, 2,750,000*l.*), with valuable privileges and property of the state,—while these dealers in treason and rebellion pocketed each from 240 to 280,000*l.* sterling! A more infamous transaction is not on record.

To carry this wicked conspiracy into effect, the English took the field against their victim Suraja Dowla; and Meer Jaffier, the traitor, in the midst of the engagement moved off, and went over to the English with his troops—thus determining the fate of a great kingdom, and of 30,000,000 of people, with the loss of twenty Europeans killed and wounded, of sixteen sepoys killed, and only 36 wounded. The unfortunate prince was soon afterwards seized and assassinated by the son of this traitor Meer Jaffier. The vices and inefficiency of this bad man soon compelled the English to pull him down from the throne into which they had so criminally raised him. They then set up in his stead his son-in-law, Meer Causim. This man for a time served their purpose, by the activity with which he raised money to pay their claims upon him. He resorted to every species of cruelty and injustice to extort the necessary funds from his unfortunate subjects. But about three years, nearly the same period as their former puppet-nabob had reigned, sufficed to weary them of him. He was rigorous enough to raise money to pay them, but he was not tool enough, when that was done, to humour every scheme of rapacity which they dictated to him. They complained of his not allowing their goods to pass duty-free through his territories; he therefore abolished all duties, and thus laid open the trade to everybody. This enraged them, and they determined to depose him. Meer Causim, however, was not so readily dismissed as Meer Jaffier had been. He resisted vigorously; massacred such of their troops as fell into his hands, and fleeing into Oude, brought them into war with its nabob. What is most remarkable, they again set up old Meer Jaffier, whom they had before deposed for his crimes and his imbecility. But probably, from their experience of Meer Causim, they now preferred an easy tool to one with more self-will. In their treaty with him they made a claim upon him for ten lacs of rupees; which demand speedily grew to 20, 30, 40, and finally to 53 lacs of rupees. All delicacy was laid aside in soliciting the payment, and one half of it was soon extorted from him. The Subahdar, in fact, was now become the merest puppet in their hands. They were the real lords of Bengal, and in direct receipt of more than half the revenues. Within less than ten years from the disgraceful bargain with the traitor Meer Jaffier, they had made Bengal their own, though they still hesitated to avow themselves as its sovereigns; they had got possession of Benares; they had acquired that power over the Nabob of Oude, in consequence of the successful war brought upon him by his alliance with the deposed nabob Meer Causim, that would at any time make them entirely his masters; the Mogul himself was ready and anxious to obtain their friendship; they were, in short, become the far greatest power in India.

Here then is an opening instance of the means by which we acquired our territories in India; and the language of Lord Clive, when he returned thither as governor of Bengal in 1765, may shew that other scenes were likely to ensue. "We have at last arrived at that critical period which I have long foreseen; I mean that period which renders it necessary for us to determine whether we can or shall take the whole to ourselves. Jaffier Ali Khan is dead. His natural son is a minor; but I know not whether he is yet declared successor. Sujah Dowla is beat from his dominions. We are in possession of them; and it is scarcely hyperbole to say—to-morrow the whole Mogul empire is in our power. The inhabitants of the country, we know by long experience, have no attachment to any obligation. Their forces are neither disciplined, commanded, nor paid like ours. Can it then be doubtful that a large army of Europeans will effectually preserve us sovereigns?"

The scene of aggression and aggrandizement here indicated, soon grew so wide and busy, that it would far exceed the whole space of this narrative to trace even rapidly its great outlines. The Great Mogul, the territories of Oude and Arcot, Mysore, Travancore, Benares, Tanjore, the Mahrattas, the whole peninsula in fact, speedily felt the effect of these views, in diplomatic or military subjection. We can point out no fortunate exception, and must therefore content ourselves with briefly touching upon some of the more prominent cases.

The first thing that deserves attention, is the treatment of the Mogul himself. This is the statement of it by the French historian: "The Mogul having been driven out of Delhi by the Pattans, by whom his son had been set up in his room, was wandering from one province to another in search of a place of refuge in his own territories, and requesting succour from his own vassals, but without success. Abandoned by his subjects, betrayed by his allies, without support and without an army, he was allured by the power of the English, and implored their protection. They promised to conduct him to Delhi, and re-establish him on his throne; but they insisted that he should previously cede to them the absolute sovereignty over Bengal. This cession was made by an authentic act, attended by all the formalities usually practised throughout the Mogul empire. The English, possessed of this title, which was to give a kind of legitimacy to their usurpation, at least in the eyes of the vulgar, soon forgot the promises they had made. They gave the Mogul to understand, that particular circumstances would not suffer them to be concerned in such an enterprise; but some better opportunity was to be hoped for; and to make up for his losses, they assigned him a pension of six millions of rupees (262,500*l.*) with the revenue of Allahabad, and Sha Ichanabad, or Delhi, upon which that unfortunate prince was reduced to subsist himself, in one of the principal towns of Benares, where he had taken up his residence."—*Raynal.*

Hastings, in fact, made it a reason for depriving him again even of this pension, that he had sought the aid of the Mahrattas, to do that which he had vainly hoped from the English—to restore him to his throne. This is Mills's relation of this fact, founded on the fifth Parliamentary Report.—"Upon receiving from him the grant of the duannee, or the receipt and management of the revenues of Bengal, Bahar, and Orissa, it was agreed that, as the royal share of these revenues, twenty-six lacs of rupees should be annually paid to him by the Company. His having accepted of the assistance of the Mahrattas to place him on the throne of his ancestors, was now made use of as a reason for telling him, that the tribute of these provinces should be paid to him no more. Of the honour, or the discredit, however, of this transaction, the principal share belongs not to the governor, but to the Directors themselves, who, in their letter to Bengal, of the 11th of November 1768, had said, 'If the emperor flings himself into the hands of the Mahrattas, or any other power, we are disengaged from him, *and it may open a fair opportunity of withholding* the 26 lacs we now pay him.'" Upon the whole, indeed, of the measure dealt out to this unhappy sovereign,—depriving him of the territories of Corah and Allahabad; depriving him of the tribute which was due to him from these provinces of his which they possessed —the Directors bestowed unqualified approbation; and though they condemned the use which had been made of their troops in subduing the country of the Rohillas, they frankly declare, "We, upon the maturest deliberation, confirm the treaty of Benares." "Thus," adds Mills, "they had plundered the unhappy Emperor of 26 lacs per annum, and the two provinces of Corah and Allahabad, which they had sold to the Vizir for 50 lacs of rupees, on the plea that he had forfeited them by his alliance with the Mahrattas;" as though he was not free, if one party would not assist him to regain his rights, to seek that assistance from another.

Passing over the crooked policy of the English, in seizing upon the isles of Salsette and Bassein, near Bombay, and treating for them afterwards, and all the perfidies of the war for the restoration of Ragabah, the Peishwa of the Mahrattas, the fate of the Nabob of Arcot, one of their earliest allies, is deserving of particular notice, as strikingly exemplifying their policy. They began by obtaining a grant of land in 1750, surrounding Madras. They then were only too happy to assist the Nabob against the French. For these military aids, in which Clive distinguished himself, the English took good care to stipulate for their usually monstrous payments. Mahomed Ali, the nabob, soon found that he was unable to satisfy the demands of his allies. They urged upon him the maintenance of large bodies of troops for the defence of his territories against these French and other enemies. This threw him still more inextricably into debt, and therefore more inextricably into their power. He became an unresisting tool in their hands. In his name the most savage exactions were practised on his subjects. The whole revenues of his kingdom, however, proved totally inadequate to the perpetually accumulating demands upon them. He borrowed money where he could, and at whatever interest, of the English themselves. When this interest could not be paid, he made over to them, under the name of *tuncaus,* the revenues of some portion of his domains. These assignments directly decreasing his resources, only raised the demands of his other creditors more violently, and the fleecing of his subjects became more and more dreadful. In this situation, he began to cast his eyes on the neighbouring states, and to incite his allies, by the assertion of various claims upon them, to join him in falling upon them, and thus to give him an opportunity of paying them. This exactly suited their views. It gave them a prospect of money, and of conquest too, under the plausible colour of assisting their ally in urging his just claims. They first joined him in falling on the Rajah of Tanjore, whom the Nabob claimed as a tributary, and indebted to him in a large amount of revenue. The Rajah was soon reduced to submission, and agreed to pay 30 lacs and 50,000 rupees, and to aid the Nabob in all his wars. Scarcely, however, was this treaty signed, than they repented of it; thought they had not got enough; hoped the Rajah would not be exact to a day in his payment, in which case they would fall on him again for breach of treaty. It so happened;—they rushed out of their camp, seized on part of Vellum, and the districts of Coiladdy and Elangad, to the retention of which the poor Rajah was obliged to submit.

This affair being so fortunately adjusted, the Nabob called on his willing allies to attack the Marawars. They, too, he said, owed him money; and money was what the English were always in want of. They readily assented, though they declared that they believed the Nabob to have no real claim on the Marawars whatever. But then, they said, the Nabob has made them his enemies, and it is necessary for his security that they should be reduced. They did not pretend it was just—but then, it was politic. The particulars of this war are barbarous and disgraceful to the English. The Nabob thirsted for the destruction of these states: he and his Christian allies soon reduced Ramnadaporam, the capital of the great Marawar, seized the Polygar, a minor of twelve years old, his mother, and the Duan; they came suddenly upon the Polygar of the lesser Marawar while he was trusting to a treaty just made, and killed him; and pursued the inhabitants of the country with severities that can only be represented by the language of one of the English officers addressed to the Council. Speaking of the animosity of the people against them, and their attacking the baggage, he says, "I can only determine it by reprisals, which will oblige me to plunder and burn the villages, kill every man in them, and take prisoners the women and children. These are actions which the nature of this war will require."—*Tanjore Papers.*

Such were the unholy deeds into which the Nabob and the great scheme of acquisition of territory had led our countrymen in 1773; but this was only the beginning of these affairs. This bloody campaign ended, and large sums of money levied, the Nabob proposed *another* war on the Rajah of Tanjore! There was not the remotest plea of injury from the Rajah, or breach of treaty. He had paid the enormous sum demanded of him before, by active levies on his subjects, and by mortgaging lands and jewels; but the Nabob had now made him a very dangerous enemy—he *might* ally himself with Hyder Ali, or the French, or some power or other—therefore it was better that he should be utterly destroyed, and his country put into the power of the Nabob! "Never," exclaims Mr. Mills, "I suppose, was the resolution taken to make war upon a lawful sovereign, with a view of reducing him entirely, that is, stripping him of his dominions, and either putting him and his family to death, or making them prisoners for life, upon a more accommodating reason! We have done the Rajah great injury—we have no intention of doing him right—this is a sufficient reason for going on to his destruction." But it was not only thought, but done; and this was the bargain: The Nabob was to advance money and all due necessaries for the war, and to pay 10,000 instead of 7,000 sepoys. The unhappy Rajah was speedily defeated, and taken prisoner with his family; and his country put into the hands of his mortal enemy. There were men of honour and virtue enough amongst the Directors at home, however, to feel a proper disgust, or at least, regard for public opinion, at these unprincipled proeeedings, and the Rajah, through the means of Lord Paget, was restored, not however without having a certain quantity of troops quartered upon him; a yearly payment of four lacs of pagodas imposed; and being bound not to make any treaty or assist any power without the consent of the English. He was, in fact, put into the first stage of that process of subjection which would, in due time, remove from him even the shadow of independence.

Such were the measures by which the Nabob of Arcot endeavoured to relieve himself from his embarrassments with the English; but they would not all avail. Their demands grew faster than he could find means to satisfy them. Their system of action was too well devised to fail them; their victims rarely escaped from their toils: he might help them to ruin his neighbours, but he could not escape them himself. During his life he was surrounded by a host of cormorant creditors; his country, harassed by perpetual exactions, rapidly declined; and the death of his son and successor, Omdut-ul-Omrah, in 1801, produced one of the strangest scenes in this strange history. The Marquis Wellesley was then Governor-general, and, pursuing that sweeping course which stripped away the hypocritical mask from British power in India, threw down so many puppet princes, and displayed English dominion in Hindostan in its gigantic nakedness. The revenues of the Carnatic had been before taken in the hands of the English, but Lord Wellesley resolved to depose the prince; and the manner in which this deposition was effected, was singularly despotic and unfeeling. They had come to the resolution to depose the Nabob, and only looked about for some plausible pretence. This they professed to have found in a correspondence which, by the death of Tippoo Saib, had fallen into their hands—a correspondence between Tippoo and some officers of the Nabob. They alleged that this correspondence contained injurious and even treasonable language towards the English. When, therefore, the Nabob lay on his death-bed, they surrounded his house with troops, and immediately that the breath had departed from him they demanded to see his will. This rude and unfeeling behaviour, so repugnant to the ideas of every people, however savage and brutal, at a moment so solemn and sacred to domestic sorrow, was respectfully protested against—but in vain. The will they insisted upon seeing, and accordingly the will was put into their hands by the son of the Nabob, now about to mount the throne himself. Finding that the son was nominated as his heir and successor by the Nabob, the Commissioners immediately announced to him the charge of treason against his father, and that the throne was thereby forfeited by the family. This charge, of course, was a matter of surprise to the family; especially when the papers said to contain the treason were produced, and they could find in them nothing but terms of fidelity and respect towards the English government. But the English had resolved that the charge should be a sufficient charge, and the young prince manfully resisting it, they then declared him to be of illegitimate birth,—a very favourite and convenient plea with them. On this they set him aside, and made a treaty with another prince, in which, for a certain provision, the Carnatic was made over to them for ever. The young Nabob, Ali Hussein, did not long survive this scene of indignity and arbitrary deposition—his death occurring in the spring of the following year.

Such was the English treatment of their friend the Nabob of Arcot;—the Nabob of Arcot, whose name was for years continually heard in England as the powerful ally of the British, as their coadjutor against the French, against the ambitious Hyder Ali, as their zealous and accommodating friend on all occasions. It was in vain that either the old Nabob, or the young one, whom they so summarily deposed, pleaded the faith of treaties, their own hereditary right, or ancient friendship. Arcot had served its turn; it had been the stalking-horse to all the aggressions on other states that they needed from it,—they had exacted all that could be exacted in the name of the Nabob from his subjects—they had squeezed the sponge dry; and moreover the time was now come that they could with impunity throw off the stealthy crouching attitude of the tiger, the smiling meek mask of alliance, and boldly seize upon undisguised sovereign powers in India. Arcot was but one state amongst many that were now to be so treated. Benares, Oude, Tanjore, Surat, and others found themselves in the like case.

Benares had been a tributary of Oude; but in 1764, when the English commenced war against the Nabob of Oude, the Rajah of Benares joined the English, and rendered them the most essential services. For these he was taken under the English protection. At first with so much delicacy and consideration was he treated, that a resident was not allowed, as in the case of other tributaries, to reside in his capital, lest in the words of the minute of the Governor-general in command in 1775:—"such resident might acquire an improper influence over the Rajah and his country, which would in effect render him master of both; lest it should end," as they knew that such things as a matter of course did end, "in reducing him to the mean and depraved state of a mere Zemindar." The council expressed its anxiety that the Rajah's independence should be in no way compromised than by the mere fact of the payment of his tribute, which, says Mills, continued to be paid with an exactness rarely exemplified in the history of the tributary princes of Hindostan. But unfortunately, the Rajah gave some offence to the powerful Warren Hastings, and there was speedily a requisition made upon him for the maintenance of three battalions of sepoys, estimated at five lacs of rupees. The Rajah pleaded inability to pay it forthwith; but five days only were given him. This was followed by a third and fourth requisition of the same sort. Seeing how the tide was running against him, the unhappy Rajah sent a private gift of two lacs of rupees to Mr. Hastings,—the pretty sum of 20,000*l*., in the hope of regaining his favour, and stopping this ruinous course of exaction. That unprincipled man took the money, but exacted the payment of the public demand with unabated rigour, and even fined him 10,000*l*. for delay in payment, and ordered troops, as he had done before, to march into his country to enforce the iniquitous exaction!

The work of diplomatic robbery on the Rajah now went on rapidly. "The screw was now turned" with vigour,—to use a homely but expressive phrase, the nose was held desperately to the grindstone. No bounds were set to the pitiless fury of spoliation, for the Governor's revenge had none; and besides, there was a dreadful want of money to defray the expenses of the wars with Hyder into which the government had plunged. "I was resolved," says Hastings, "to draw from his guilt" (his having offended Mr. Hastings—the guilt was all on the other side) "the means of relief to the Company's distresses. In a word, I had determined to make him pay largely for his pardon, or to exact a severe vengeance for his past delinquency." What this delinquency could possibly be, unless it were not having sent Mr. Hastings a *second* present of *two lacs*, is not to be discovered; but the success of the first placebo was not such as to elicit a second. The Rajah, therefore, tried what effect he could produce upon the council at large; he sent an offer of TWENTY LACS *for the public service.* It was scornfully rejected, and a demand of FIFTY *lacs* was made! The impossibility of compliance with such extravagant demands was what was anticipated; the Governor hastened to Benares, arrested the Rajah in his own capital; set at defiance the indignation of the people at this insult. The astounded Rajah made his escape, but only to find himself at war with his insatiable despoilers. In vain did he propose every means of accommodation. Nothing would now serve but his destruction. He was attacked, and compelled to fly. Bidgegur, where, says Hastings himself, "he had left his wife, a woman of amiable character, his mother, all the other women of his family, and the survivors of the family of his father, Bulwant Sing," was obliged to capitulate; and Hastings, in his fell and inextinguishable vengeance, even, says Mills, "in his letters to the commanding officer, employed expressions which implied that the plunder of these women was the due reward of the soldiers; which suggested one of the most dreadful outrages to which, in the conception of the country, a human being could be exposed."

The fort was surrendered on express stipulation for the safety and freedom from search, of the females; but adds Mills, "the idea suggested by Mr. Hastings diffused itself but too perfectly amongst the soldiery; and when the princesses, with their relatives and attendants, to the number of three hundred women, besides children, withdrew from the castle, the capitulation was shamefully violated; they were plundered of their effects, and their persons otherwise rudely and disgracefully treated by the licentious people, and followers of the camp." He adds, "one is delighted, for the honour of distinguished gallantry, that in no part of the opprobrious business the commanding officer had any share. He leaned to generosity and the protection of the princesses from the beginning. His utmost endeavours were exerted to restrain the outrages of the camp; and he represented them with feeling to Mr. Hastings, who expressed his concurrence, etc."

The only other consolation in this detestable affair is, that the soldiers, in spite of Hastings, got the plunder of the Rajah, and that the Court of Directors at home censured his conduct. But these are miserable drops of satisfaction in this huge and overflowing cup of bitterness, —of misery to trusting, friendly, and innocent people; and of consequent infamy on the British name.

We must, out of the multitudes of such cases, confine ourselves to one more. The atrocities just recited had put Benares into the entire power of the English, but it had only tended to increase the pecuniary difficulties. The soldiery had got the plunder—the expenses of the war were added to the expenses of other wars;—some other kingdom must be plundered, for booty must be had: so Mr. Hastings continued his journey, and paid a visit to the Nabob of Oude. It is not necessary to trace the complete progress of this Nabob's friendship with the English. It was exactly like that of the other princes just spoken of. A treaty was made with him; and then from time to time, the usual exactions of money and the maintenance of troops for his subjection were heaped upon him. As with the Nabob of Arcot, so with him, they were ready to sanction and assist him in his most criminal views on his neighbours, to which his need of money drove him. He proposed to Mr. Hastings, in 1773, to assist him *in exterminating the Rohillas*, a people bordering on his kingdom; "a people," says Mills, "whose territory was, by far, the best governed part of India; the people protected, their industry encouraged, and the country flourishing beyond all parallel." It was by a careful neutrality, and by these acts, that the Rohillas sought to maintain their independence; and it was of such a people that Hastings, sitting at table with his tool the Nabob of Oude, coolly heard him offer him a bribe of forty lacs of rupees (400,000*l.*) and the payment of the troops furnished, to assist him to destroy them utterly! There does not seem to have existed in the mind of Hastings one human feeling: a proposition which would have covered almost any other man with unspeakable horror, was received by him as a matter of ordinary business. "Let us see," said Hastings, "we have a heavy bonded debt, at one time 125 lacs of rupees. By this a saving of nearly one third of our military expenses would be effected during the period of such service; the forty lacs would be an ample supply to our treasury; and the Vizir (the Nabob of Oude) would be freed from a troublesome neighbour." These are the monster's own words; the bargain was struck, but it was agreed to be kept secret from the council and court of Directors. In one of Hastings' letters, still extant, he tells the Nabob, "should the Rohillas be guilty of a breach of their agreement, (a demand of forty lacs suddenly made upon them—for in this vile affair everything had a ruffian character—they first demanded their money, and then murdered them), *we will thoroughly exterminate them*, and settle your excellency in the country." The extermination was conducted to the letter, as agreed, as far as was in their power. The Rohillas defended themselves most gallantly; but were overpowered,—and their chief, and upwards of a hundred thousand people fled to the mountains. The whole country lay at the mercy of the allies, and the British officers themselves declared that perhaps never were the rights of conquest more savagely abused. Colonel Champion, one of them, says in a letter of June 1774, published in the fifth Parliamentary Report, App. 21, "the inhumanity and dishonour with which the late proprietors of this country and their families have been used, is known all over these parts. A relation of them would swell this letter to an enormous size. I could not help compassionating such unparalleled misery, and my requests to the Vizir to shew lenity were frequent, but as fruitless as even those advices which I almost hourly gave him with regard to the destruction of the villages; with respect to which he always promised fair, but did not observe one of his promises, nor cease to overspread the country with flames, till three days after the fate of Hafez Rhamet was decided." The Nabob had frankly and repeatedly assured Hastings that his intention was to *exterminate* the Rohillas, and every one who bore the name of Rohilla was either butchered, or found his safety in flight and in exile. Such were the diabolical deeds into which our government drove the native princes, by their enormous exactions, or encouraged them in, only in the end to enslave them the more.

Before the connexion between the English and Oude, its revenues had exceeded 3,000,000*l.* sterling, and was levied without being accused of deteriorating the country. In the year 1779, it did not exceed one half of that sum, and in the subsequent years it fell far below it, while the rate of taxation was increased, and the country exhibited every mark of oppressive exaction. In this year the Nabob represented to the council the wretched condition to which he was reduced by their exactions: that the children of the deceased Nabob had subsisted in a very distressed manner for two years past; that the attendants, writers, and servants, had received no pay for that period; that his father's private creditors were daily pressing him, and there was not a foot of country which could be appropriated to their payment;

that the revenue was deficient fifteen lacs (1,500,000*l.* sterling); that the country and cultivation were abandoned; the old chieftains and useful attendants of the court were forced to leave it; that the Company's troops were not only useless, but caused great loss to the revenue and confusion in the country; and that the support of his household, on the meanest scale, was beyond his power.

This melancholy representation produced—what?—pity, and an endeavour to relieve the Nabob?—no, exasperation. Mr. Hastings declared that, both it and the crisis in which it was made were equally alarming. The only thing thought of was what was to be done if the money did not come in? But Mr. Hastings, on his visit to the Nabob at Lucknow, made a most lucky discovery. He found that the mother and widow of the late Nabob were living there, and possessed of immense wealth. His rapacious mind, bound by no human feeling or moral principle, and fertile in schemes of acquisition, immediately conceived the felicitous design of setting the Nabob to strip those ladies, well known to English readers since the famous trial of Mr. Hastings, as "the Begums." It was agreed between the Nabob and Mr. Hastings, that his Highness should be relieved of the expense which he was unable to bear, of the English troops and gentlemen; and he, on his part, engaged to strip the Begums of both their treasure and their jaghires (revenues of certain lands), delivering to the Governor-general the proceeds. As a plea for this most abominable transaction, in which a prince was compelled by his cruel necessities and the grinding exactions and threats of the English to pillage forcibly his near relatives, a tale of treason was hatched against these poor women. When they refused to give up their money, the chief eunuchs were put to the torture till the ladies in compassion gave way: 550,000*l.* sterling were thus forced from them: the torture was still continued, in hope of extracting more: the women of the Zenana were deprived of food at various times till they were on the point of perishing for want; and every expedient was tried that the most devilish invention could suggest, till it was found that they had really drawn the last doit from them. But what more than all moves one's indignation against this base English inquisitor, was, that he received as his share of these spoils the sum of ten lacs, or 100,000*l.*!—and that notwithstanding the law of the Company against the receipt of presents; its avowed distress for want of money; and the poverty of the kingdom of Oude, which was thus plundered and disgraced from the very inability to pay its debts, if debts such shameful exactions can be called,—Hastings did not hesitate to apprise the council of what he had received, and requested their permission to retain it for himself.

Of the numerous transactions of a most wicked character connected with these affairs; of the repugnance of the Nabob to do the dirty work of Hastings on his relatives, the Begums; of the haughty insolence by which his tyrant compelled him to the compact; of the restoration of the jaghires, but not the moneys of the Begums; of the misery and desolation which forced itself even upon the horny eyes of Hastings as he made his second progress through the territories of Oude, the work of his own oppressions and exactions; of the 12,500,000*l.* which he added by his wars and political manœuvres to the Indian debt—we have not here room to note more than the existence of such facts, which are well known to all the readers of Indian history, or of the trial of Warren Hastings, where every artifice of the lawyers was employed to prevent the evidence of these things being brought forward; and where a House of Peers was found base or weak enough to be guided by such artifices, to refuse the most direct evidence against the most atrocious transaction in history; and thus to give sanction and security to the commission of the most dreadful crimes and cruelties in our distant colonies. Nothing could increase from this time the real power of the

English over Oude, though circumstances might occasion a more open avowal of it. Even during the government of Lord Cornwallis and Sir John Shore, now Lord Teignmouth, two of the most worthy and honourable rulers that British India ever had, the miseries and exactions continued, and the well-intentioned financial measures of Lord Cornwallis even tended to increase them. In 1798, the governor, Sir John Shore, proceeded to depose the ruling Nabob as illegitimate (a plea on which the English set aside a number of Indian princes), and elevated another in his place, and that upon evidence, says the historian, "upon which an English court of law would not have decided against him a question of a few pounds."

It was not, however, till 1799, under the government of the Marquis Wellesley, that the hand of British power was stretched to the utmost over this devoted district. That honest and avowed usurper, who disdained the petty acts of his predecessors, but declared that the British dominion over the peninsula of India must be frankly avowed, and fearlessly asserted—certainly a much better doctrine than the cowardly and hypocritical one hitherto acted upon;—that every Englishman who did not belong to the Company must and should be expelled from that country; and that the English power and the Corporate monopoly should be so strenuously and unflinchingly exerted, that foreign aggression or domestic complaint should be alike dispersed;—this straightforward Governor-general soon drove the Nabob of Oude to such desperation, by the severity of his measures and exactions, that he declared his wish to abdicate. Nothing could equal the joy of the Governor-general at the prospect of this easy acquisition of this entire territory: but that joy was damped by discovering that the Nabob only wished to resign in favour of—his own son! The chagrin of the Governor-general on this discovery is not to be expressed; and the series of operations then commenced to force the Nabob to abdicate in favour of the Company;

when that could not be effected, to compel him to sacrifice one half of his territories to save the rest; when that sacrifice was made, to inform him that he was to have no independent power in his remaining half—is one of the most instructive lessons in the art of diplomatic fleecing, of forcing a man out of his own by the forms of treaty but with the iron hand of irresistible power, which any despot who wishes to do a desperate deed handsomely, and in the most approved style, can desire. It was in vain that the Nabob declared his payment of exactions; his hereditary right; his readiness shewn on all occasions to aid and oblige; the force of treaties in his favour. It was in vain that he asked to what purpose should he give up one half of his dominions if he were not to have power over the other, when it was to secure this independent power that he gave up that half? What are all the arguments of right, justice, reason, or humanity, when Ahab wants the vineyard of Naboth, and the Jezebel of political and martial power tells him that he will give it him? The fate of Oude was predetermined, along with that of various other states, by the Governor-general, and it was decided as he determined it should be.

Before we close this chapter, we will give one instance of the manner in which the territories of those who held aloof, and did not covet the fatal friendship of the English, were obtained, and the most striking of these are the dominions of Hyder Ali—the kingdom of Mysore.

Hyder was a soldier of fortune. He had risen by an active and enterprising disposition from the condition of a common soldier to the head of the state. The English considered him as an ambitious, able, and therefore very dangerous person in India. There can be no doubt that he considered them the same. He was an adventurer; so were they. He had acquired a great territory by means that would not bear the strictest scrutiny; so had they;—but there was this difference between them, Hyder acted according to the customs and maxims in which he had been educated, and which he saw universally practised by all the princes around him. He neither had the advantages of Christian knowledge and principle, nor pretended to them. The English, on the contrary, came there as merchants; they were continually instructed by their masters at home not to commit military aggressions. They were bound by the laws of their country not to do it. They professed to be in possession of a far higher system of religion and morals than Hyder and his people had. They pretended to be the disciples of the Prince of Peace. Their magnanimous creed they declared to be, "To do to others as they would wish to be done by." But neither Hyder nor any other Indian ever saw the least evidence of any such superiority of morals, or of faith in their conduct. They were as ambitious, and far more greedy of money than the heathen that they pretended to despise for their heathenism. They ought to have set a better example—but they did not. There never was a people that grasped more convulsively at dominion, or were less scrupulous in the means of obtaining it. They declared Hyder cruel and perfidious. He knew them to be both. This was the ground on which they stood. There were reasons why the English should avoid interfering with Hyder. There were none why he should avoid encroaching on them, for he did not profess any such grand principles of action as they did. If they were what they pretended to be, they ought to preach peace and union amongst the Indian princes: but union was of all things in the world the very one which they most dreaded; for they *were not* what they pretended to be; but sought on the divisions of the natives to establish their own power. Had Hyder attacked them in their own trading districts, there could have been no reason why they should not chastise him for it. But it does not appear that he ever did attack them at all till they fell upon him, and that with the avowed intention to annihilate his power as dangerous. No, say they, but he attacked the territories of our ally the

Subahdar of Deccan, which we were bound to defend. And here it is that we touch again upon that subtle policy by which it became impossible, when they had once got a footing in the country that, having the will and the power, they should not eventually have the dominion. While professing to avoid conquest, we have seen that they went on continually making conquests. But it was always on the plea of aiding their allies. They entered knowingly into alliances on condition of defending with arms their allies, and then, when they committed aggressions, it was *for* these allies. In the end the allies were themselves swallowed up, with all the additional territories thus gained. It was a system of fattening allies, as we fatten oxen, till they were more worthy of being devoured. They cast their subtle threads of policy like the radiating filaments of the spider's web, till the remotest extremity of India could not be touched without startling them from their concealed centre into open day, ready to run upon the unlucky offender. It was utterly impossible, on such a system, but that offences should come, and wo to them by whom they did come.

The English were unquestionably the aggressors in the hostilities with Hyder. They entered into a treaty with Nizam Ali, the Subahdar of Deccan, offensive and defensive; and the very first deed which they were to do, was to seize the fort of Bangalore, which belonged to Hyder. They had actually marched in 1767, into his territories, when Hyder found means to draw the Nizam from his alliance, and in conjunction with him fell upon them, and compelled them to fly to Trincomalee. By this unprovoked and voluntary act they found themselves involved at once in a war with a fierce and active enemy, who pursued them to the very walls of Madras; scoured the country with his cavalry; and compelled them to a dishonourable peace in 1769, by which they bound themselves to assist *him* too in his defensive wars! To enter voluntarily into such conditions with such a man, betrayed no great delicacy of moral feeling as to what wars they engaged in, or no great honesty in their intentions as regarded the treaty itself. They must soon either fight with some of Hyder's numerous enemies, or break faith with him. Accordingly the very next year the Mahrattas invaded his territories; he called earnestly on his English allies for aid, and aid they did not give. Hyder had now the justest reason to term them perfidious, and to hold them in distrust. Yet, though deeply exasperated by this treachery, he would in 1778 most willingly have renewed his alliance with them; and the presidency of Madras acknowledged their belief that, had not the treaty of 1769 been evaded, Hyder would never have sought other allies than themselves. There were the strongest reasons why they should have cultivated an amicable union with him, both to withdraw him from the French, and on account of his own great power and revenues. But they totally neglected him, or insulted him with words of mere cold courtesy; and a new aggression upon the fortress of Mahè, a place tributary to Hyder, which they attacked in order to expel the French, and which Hyder resented on the same principle as they would resent an attack upon any tributary of their own, well warranted the declaration of Hyder, that they "were the most faithless and usurping of mankind." They were these arbitrary and impolitic deeds which brought down Hyder speedily upon them, with an army 100,000 strong; and soon shewed them Madras menaced, the Carnatic overrun, Arcot taken, and a war of such a desperate and bloody character raging around them, as they had never yet seen in India, and which might probably have expelled them thence, had not death released them in 1782 from so formidable a foe, who had been so wantonly provoked.

Tippoo Sultaun, with all his activity and cunning, had not the masterly military genius of his father,—but he possessed all the fire of his resentment, and it was not to be expected that, after what had passed, there could be much interval of irritation between him and the English. They had roused Hyder as a lion is roused from his den, and he made them feel his power. They would naturally look on his son with suspicion, and Tippoo had been taught to regard them as "the most faithless and usurping of mankind." Whatever, therefore, may be said for or against him, on the breaking out of the second war with him, the original growth of hostility between the British and the Mysorean monarchs, must be charged to the former, and in the case of the last war, there appears to have been no real breach of treaty on the part of Tippoo. He had been severely punished for any act of irritation which he might have committed against any of the British allies, by the reduction of his capital, the surrender of his sons as hostages, and the stripping away of one half of his territories to be divided among his enemies, each of whom had enriched himself with half a million sterling of annual revenue at his expense. Tippoo must have been nothing less than a madman in his shattered condition, and with his past experience, to have lightly ventured on hostilities with the English. But it was charged on him that he was seeking an alliance with the French. What then? He had the clearest right so to do. So long as he maintained the terms of his treaty, the English had no just right to violate theirs towards him. The French were his ancient and hereditary friends. Tippoo persisted to the last that he had done nothing to warrant an attack upon him. But Lord Mornington had adopted his notions about consolidating the British power in India, and every possible circumstance, or suspicion of a circumstance, was to be seized upon as a plea for carrying his plans into effect. It was enough that a fear *might* be entertained of Tippoo's designs. It became good policy to get the start; and when once that forestalling system in hostilities, that outstripping in the race of mischief, is adopted, there is no possible violence nor enormity which may not be undertaken, or defended upon it. Tippoo was assailed by the British, and their ally the Nizam; and though he again and again protested his innocence, again and again asked for peace, he was pursued to his capital, and killed whilst bravely defending it. His territories were then divided amongst those who had divided the former half of them in like manner,—the English, the Nizam, and the Mahrattas,—with a little state appropriated to a puppet-rajah. Thus did the English shew what they would do to those who dared to decline their protection. Thus did they pursue, beat down, and destroy with all their mighty resources, an independent prince, whose whole revenue, after their first partition of his realm, did not much exceed a million sterling. We have heard a vast deal in Europe of the partition of Poland, but how much better was the forcible dismemberment of Mysore? The injury of this dismemberment of his kingdom is however not the least heaped upon Tippoo. On his name have been heaped all the odious crimes that make us hate the worst of tyrants. Cruelty, perfidy, low cunning, and all kinds of baseness, make up the idea of Tippoo which we have derived from those who profited by his destruction. But what say the most candid historians? "That the accounts which we have received from our countrymen, who dreaded and feared him, are marked with exaggeration, is proved by this circumstance, that his servants adhered to him with a fidelity which those of few princes in any age or country have displayed. Of his cruelty we have heard the more, because our own countrymen were amongst the victims of it. But it is to be observed, that unless in certain instances, the proof of which cannot be regarded as better than doubtful, their sufferings, however intense, were only the sufferings of a very rigorous imprisonment, of which, considering the manner in which it is lavished upon them by their own laws, Englishmen ought not to be very forward to complain. At that very time, in the dungeons of Madras or Calcutta, it is probable that unhappy sufferers were enduring calamities for debts of 100*l.* not less atrocious than those which Tippoo, a prince born and educated in a barbarous country, and ruling over a barbarous people, inflicted upon imprisoned enemies, part of a nation who, by the evils they had brought upon him, exasperated him almost to frenzy, and whom he regarded as the enemies both of God and man. Besides, there is among the papers relating to the intercourse of Tippoo with the French, a remarkable proof of his humanity, which, when these papers are ransacked for matters to criminate him, ought not to be suppressed. In a draught of conditions on which he desired to form a treaty with them, these are the words of a distinct article :—'I demand that male and female prisoners, as well English as Portuguese, who shall be taken by the republican troops, or by mine, shall be treated with humanity; and, with regard to their persons, that they shall (their property becoming the right of the allies) be transported, at our joint expense, out of India, to places far distant from the territories of the allies.'

"Another feature in the character of Tippoo was his religion, with a sense of which his mind was most deeply impressed. He spent a considerable part of every day in prayer. He gave to his kingdom a particular religious title, *Cudadad*, or God-given; and he lived under a peculiarly strong and operative conviction of the superintendence of a Divine Providence. To one of his French advisers, who urged him zealously to obtain the support of the Mahrattas, he replied, 'I rely solely on Providence, expecting that I shall be alone and unsupported; but God and my courage will accomplish everything.' . . . . He had the discernment to perceive, what is so generally hid from the eyes of rulers in a more enlightened state of society, that it is the prosperity of those who labour with their hands which constitutes the principle and cause of the prosperity of the states. He therefore made it his business to protect them against the intermediate orders of the community, by whom it is so difficult to prevent them from being oppressed. His country was, accordingly, at least during the first and better part of his reign, the best cultivated, and his population the most flourishing, in India: while under the English and their pageants, the population of the Carnatic and Oude, hastening to the state of deserts, was the most wretched upon the face of the earth; and even Bengal itself, under the operations of laws ill adapted to their circumstances, was suffering almost all the evils which the worst of governments could inflict. . . . . . For an eastern prince he was full of knowledge. His mind was active, acute, and ingenious. But in the value which he set upon objects, whether as means, or as an end, he was almost perpetually deceived. Besides, a conviction appears to have been rooted in his mind that the English had now formed a resolution to deprive him of his kingdom, and it was useless to negotiate, because no submission to which he could reconcile his mind, would restrain them in the gratification of their ambitious designs."—*Mills.*

Tippo was right. The great design of the English, from their first secure footing in India, was to establish their control over the whole peninsula. The French created them the most serious alarm in the progress of their career towards this object; and any native state which shewed more than ordinary energy, excited a similar feeling. For this purpose all the might of British power and policy was exerted to expel these European rivals, and to crush such more active states. The administration of the Marquis of Wellesley was the exhibition of this system full-blown. For this all the campaigns against Holkar and Scindia; the wars from north to south, and from east to west of India, were undertaken; and blood was made to flow, and debts to accumulate to a degree most monstrous. Yet the admiration of this system of policy in England has shewn how little human life and human welfare, even to this day, weigh in the scale against dominion and avarice. We hear nothing of the horrors and violence we have perpetrated, from the first invasion of Bengal, to those of Nepaul and Burmah; we have only eulogies on the empire achieved:—"See what a splendid empire we have won!" True,—there is no objection to the empire, if we could only forget the means by which it has been created. But amid all this subtle and crooked policy—this creeping into power under the colour of allies—this extortion and plunder of princes, under the name of protection—this forcible subjection and expatriation of others, we look in vain for the generous policy of the Christian merchant, and the Christian statesman.* The moderation of a Teignmouth, a Cornwallis, or a Bentinck, is deemed mere pusillanimity. Those divine maxims of peace and union which Christianity would disseminate among the natives of the countries that we visit, are condemned as the very obstacles to the growth of our power. When we exclaim, "what might not Englishmen have done in

* Sir Thomas Roe was sent in 1614, on an embassy to the Great Mogul. In his letters to the Company, he strongly advised them against the expensive ambition of acquiring territory. He tells them, "It is greater than trade can bear; for to maintain a garrison will cut out your profit: a war and traffic are incompatible. The Portuguese, notwithstanding their many rich residences, are beggared by keeping of soldiers; and yet their garrisons are but mean. They never made advantage of the Indies since they defended them;—observe this well. It has also been the error of the Dutch, who seek plantations here by the sword. They turn a wonderful stock; they prowl in all places; they possess some of the best: yet their dead pays consume all the gain. Let this be received as a rule, that if you will profit, seek it at sea and in quiet trade; for without controversy, it is an error to affect garrisons and land-wars in India."

Had Sir Thomas been inspired, could he have been a truer prophet? The East India Company, after fighting and conquering in India for two centuries, have found themselves at the dissolution of their charter, nearly fifty millions in debt; while their trade with China, a country in which they did not possess a foot of land, had become the richest commerce in the world! The article of tea alone returning between three and four millions annually, and was their sole preventive against bankruptcy. Can, indeed, any colonial acquisition be pointed out that is not a loss to the parent state?

India had they endeavoured to pacify and enlighten, instead of to exact and destroy?" we are answered by a smile, which informs us that these are but romantic notions,—that the only wisdom is to get rich!

CHAPTER II.

TREATMENT OF THE NATIVES.

Rich in the gems of India's gaudy zone,
And plunder, piled from kingdoms not their own,
Degenerate trade! thy minions could despise,
The heart-born anguish of a thousand cries;
Could lock, with impious hands their teeming store,
While famished nations died along the shore;
Could mock the groans of fellow-men; and bear
The curse of kingdoms peopled with despair;
Could stamp disgrace on man's polluted name,
And barter, with their gold, eternal shame.—*Pleasures of Hope.*

We have in some degree caught a glimpse of the subject of this chapter in the course of the last. The treatment of the native chiefs in our pursuit of territorial possession is in part the treatment of the natives, but it is unhappily a very small part. The scene of exaction, rapacity, and plunder which India became in our hands, and that upon the whole body of the population, forms one of the most disgraceful portions of human history; and while the temptations to it existed in full force, defied all the powers of legislation, or the moral influence of public opinion, to check the evil. In vain the East India Company itself, in vain the British Parliament legislated on the subject; in vain did the Court of Directors from year to year, send out the most earnest remonstrances to their servants,—the allurement was too splendid, the opportunities too seducing, the example too general, the security too great, to permit any one to attend to either law, remonstrance, or the voice of humanity. The fame of India, as a vast region of inexhaustible wealth, had resounded through the world for ages; the most astonishing notions of it floated through Europe, before the sea-tract to it was discovered; and when that was done, the marvellous fortunes made there by bold men, as it were in a single day, and by a single stroke of policy, seemed more than to warrant any previous belief. Men in power received their presents of ten, twenty, or a hundred thousand pounds. Clive, for the assistance of the British army, was presented with the magnificent gift of a jaghire, or hereditary revenue of 30,000*l.* a year! On another occasion he received his 28,000*l.*, and his fellow-rulers each a similar sum. Hastings received his twenty and his hundred thousand pounds, as familiarly as a gold snuff-box or a piece of plate would be given as a public testimony of respect for popular services in England. Every man, according to his station and his influence, found the like golden harvest. Who could avoid being inflamed with the thirst for Indian services?—who avoid the most exaggerated anticipations of fortune? It was a land, and a vast land, hedged about with laws of exclusion to all except such as went through the doors of the Company. There were there no interlopers,—no curious, because obstructed observers. There was but one object in going thither, and one interest when there. It was a soil made sacred, or rather, doomed, to the exclusive plunder of a privileged number. The highest officers in the government had the strongest motives to corruption, and therefore could by no possibility attempt to check the same corruption in those below them. When the power and influence of the Company became considerably extended over Bengal, Bahar, Orissa, Oude, the Carnatic, and Bombay, the harvest of presents grew into a most affluent one. Nothing was to be expected, no chance of justice, of attention, of alleviation from the most abominable oppression, but through the medium of presents, and those of such amounts as fairly astonish European ears. Every man, in every department, whether civil, military, or mercantile, was in the certain receipt of splendid presents. When the government had found it necessary to forbid the receipt of presents by any individual in the service, not only for themselves, but for the Company, the highest officers set the laws at defiance, and the mischief was made more secret, but not less existent.

But besides presents and official incomes, there were the farming of the revenues, and domestic trade, which opened up boundless sources of profit. The revenues were received in each district by zemindars from the ryots or husbandmen, and handed, after a fixed deduction, to the chief office of the revenue. But between these zemindars and the ryots were aumils, or other inferior officers, who farmed the revenues in each lesser district or village; that is, contracted with the zemindars for the revenues at a certain sum, and took the trouble of exacting them from the ryots, who paid a rate fixed by law or ancient custom, and could not be turned out of their lands while such rate was regularly paid. Wherever the English obtained a claim over the revenues of a prince, which we have seen they speedily did, they soon became the zemindars, or their agents, the aumils, or other middlemen between them and the ryots. Anciently, the ryots paid one-tenth of their produce, for all their taxes were paid in kind, but in time the rate grew to more than half. When the English power become more fixed and open, and it was found that under the native zemindars the exactions of the revenues did not at all satisfy their demands, they took on themselves the whole business of collecting these revenues. This, as we shall see, on the evidence of the Company's own officers, became a dreadful system to the people. The Mahomedan exactions had been generally regarded more considerate than those of the native Hindu chiefs; but the grinding pressure of the English system brought on the unfortunate ryot the most unexampled misery. Of this, however, anon. It only requires here to be pointed out as one of the various sources of enormous profits and jobbing which made India so irresistibly attractive to Englishmen.

The private trade was another grand source of revenue. The public trade, that is, the transit of goods to and from Europe, was the peculiar monopoly of the Company; but all coasting trade—trade to and between the isles, and in the interior of India, became a monopoly of the higher servants of the Company, who were at once engaged in the Company's concerns and their own. The monopoly of salt, opium, betel, and other commodities became a mine of wealth. The Company's servants could fix the price at whatever rate they pleased, and thus enhance it to the unfortunate people so as to occasion them the most intense distress. Fortunes were made in a day by this monopoly, and without the advance of a single shilling. The very Governor-general himself engaged in this private trade; and contracts were given to favourites on such terms, that two or three fortunes were made out of them before they reached the merchant. In one case that came out on the trial of Warren Hastings, a contract for opium had been given to Mr. Sullivan, though he was going into quite a different part of India, and on public business; this of course he sold again, to Mr. Benn, for 40,000*l.*; and Mr. Benn immediately sold it again for 60,000*l.*, clearing 20,000*l.* by the mere passing of the contract from one hand to the other; and the purchaser then declared that he made a large sum by it.

All these things put together, made India the theatre of sure and splendid fortune to the adventurer, and of sore and abject misery to the native. We have only to look about us in any part of England, but especially in the metropolis, and within fifty miles round it, to see what streams of wealth have flowed into this country from India. What thousands of splendid mansions and estates are lying in view, which, when the traveller inquires their history, have been purchased by the gold of India. We are told that those days of magical accumulation of wealth are over; that this great fountain of affluence is drained comparatively dry; that fortunes are not now readily made in India; yet the Company, though they have lost their monopoly of trade, and their territories are laid open to the free observation of their countrymen, are in possession of the government with a revenue of twenty millions. But all this time, what has been doing with and for the natives. We shall see that anon; yet it may here be asked, What *could* be doing? For what did men go to India? For what did they endure its oppressive and often fatal climate? Was it from philanthropical or personal motives? Did they seek the good of the Indians or their own? The latter, assuredly: and it was not to be expected that the majority of men should be so high-minded or disinterested as to seek the good of others at the expense of their own. The temptations to visit India were powerful, but not the less powerful were the motives to hasten away at the very earliest possible period. It was not to be expected from human nature that the natives could be much thought of. What *has* been done for them by the devoted few, we shall recognise with delight; at present we must revert to the evil influences of nearly two hundred years.

Amongst the first to claim our attention, are those doings in high places which have excited to strongly the cupidity of thousands, and especially those dazzling presents which became the direct causes of the most violent exactions on the people, for out of them had all these things to be drawn. The Company could, indeed, with a very bad grace, condemn bribery in its officers, for it has always been accused of this evil practice at home in order to obtain its exclusive privileges from government; and, so early as 1693, it appeared from parliamentary inquiry, that its annual expenditure under the head of gifts to men in power previous to the Revolution, seldom exceeded 1,200*l.*, but from that period to that year it had grown to nearly 90,000*l.* annually. The Duke of Leeds was impeached for a bribe of 5,000*l.*, and 10,000*l.* were even said to be traced to the king. Besides this, whenever any rival company appeared in the field, government was tempted with the loans of enormous sums, at the lowest interest. Like fruits were to be expected in India, and were not long wanting. We cannot trace this subject to its own vast extent—it would require volumes—we can only offer a few striking examples:—

None can be more remarkable than the following list, which, besides sums that we may suppose it to have been in the power of the receivers to conceal, and of the amount of which it is not easy to form a conjecture, were detected and disclosed by the Committee of the House of Commons in 1773.

The rupees are valued according to the rate of exchange of the Company's bills at the different periods.

Account of such sums as have been proved or acknowledged before the Committee to have been distributed by the Princes and other natives of Bengal, from the year 1757 *to the year* 1766, *both inclusive; distinguishing the principal times of the said distributions, and specifying the sums received by each person respectively:*—

Resolution in favour of Meer Jaffier—1757.

	Rupees.	Rupees.	£.
Mr. Drake (Governor) - -		280,000	31,500
Col. Clive, as second in the Select Committee - -	280,000		
Ditto, as Commander-in-Chief	200,000		
Ditto, as a private donation	1,600,000		
		2,080,000	234,000
Mr. Watts, as a Member of the Committee -	240,000		
Ditto, as a private donation	800,000		
		1,040,000	117,000

Resolution in favour of Meer Jaffier—1757—*continued.*

	Rupees.	£.
Major Kilpatrick - - - - -	240,000	27,000
Ditto, as a private donation - -	300,000	33,750
Mr. Maningham - - - - -	240,000	27,000
Mr. Becher - - - - - -	240,000	27,000
Six Members of Council, one lac each	600,000	68,000
Mr. Walsh - - - - - -	500,000	56,250
Mr. Scrafton - - - - - -	200,000	22,500
Mr. Lushington - - - - -	50,000	5,250
Captain Grant - - - - -	100,000	11,250
Stipulation to the Navy and Army		600,000
		1,261,075
Memorandum—the sum of two lacs to Lord Clive, as Commander-in-Chief, must be deducted from this account, it being included in the donation to the army		22,500
		1,238,575

Resolution in favour of Causim in 1760

Mr. Sumner - - - - - -		28,000
Mr. Holwell - - - - - -	270,000	30,937
Mr. M'Guire - - - - -	180,000	20,628
Mr. Smyth - - - - -	130,300	15,354
Major Yorke - - - - - -	134,000	15,354
General Caillaud - - - - -	200,000	22,916
Mr. Vansittart, 1762, received seven lacs, but the two lacs to Gen. Caillaud are included; so that only five lacs must be accounted for here - - - - -	500,000	58,333
Mr. M'Guire 5,000 gold morhs - -	75,000	8,750
		200,269

Resolution in favour of Jaffier in 1763.

Stipulation to the Army - - - -	2,500,000	291,666
Ditto to the Navy - - - - -	1,250,000	145,833
		437,499
Major Munro, in 1764, received from Bulwant Sing - - - - - -		10,000
Ditto, from the Nabob - - - -		3,000
The Officers belonging to Major Munro's family from ditto - - - - -		3,000
The Army, from the merchants at Benares	400,000	46,666
		62,666

Nudjeem-ul-Dowla's Accession, 1765.

	Rupees.	£.
Mr. Spencer - - - - - -	200,000	23,333
Messrs. Pleydell, Burdett, and Grey, one lac each - - - - - - -	300,000	35,000
Mr. Johnstone - - - - - -	237,000	27,650
Mr. Leycester - - - - - -	112,500	13,125
Mr. Senior - - - - - -	172,500	20,125
Mr. Middleton - - - - - -	122,500	14,291
Mr. Gideon Johnstone - - -	50,000	5,833
		139,357
General Carnac received from Bulwant Sing, in 1765	80,000	9,333
Ditto from the King - - - - -	200,000	23,333
Lord Clive received from the Begum, in 1766 - - - - - -	500,000	58,333
		90,999

Restitution.—Jaffier, 1757.

East India Company - - - - -	1,200,000
Europeans - - - - - -	600,000
Natives - - - - - - -	250,000
Armenians - - - - - - -	100,000
	2,150,000

Causim, 1760.

East India Company - - - - -	62,500

Jaffier, 1763.

East India Company - - - - - -	375,000
Europeans, Natives, etc. - - - - -	600,000
	975,000

Peace with Sujah Dowla.

East India Company - - -	5,000,000	583,333

Total of Presents, £2,169,665. Restitution, ect., £3,770,833.
Total amount, exclusive of Lord Clive's Jaghire, £5,940,498.

These are pretty sums to have fallen into the pockets of the English, chiefly *douceurs*, in ten years. Let the account be carried on for all India at a similar rate for a century, and what a sum! Lord Clive's jaghire alone was worth 30,000*l.* per annum. And, besides this, it appears from the above documents that he also pocketed in these transactions 292,333*l*. No wonder at the enormous fortunes rapidly made; at the enormous debts piled on the wretched nabobs, and the dreadful exactions on the still more wretched people. No man could more experimentally than Clive thus address the Directors at home, as he did in 1765: "Upon my arrival, I am sorry to say, I found your affairs in a condition so nearly desperate as would have alarmed any set of men whose sense of honour and duty to their employers had not been estranged by the too eager pursuit of their own immediate advantages. The sudden, and among many, the unwarrantable acquisition of riches (who was so entitled to say this ? had introduced luxury in every shape, and in its most pernicious excess. These two enormous evils went hand in hand together through the whole presidency, infecting almost every member of every department. Every inferior seemed to have grasped at wealth, that he might be enabled to assume that spirit of profusion which was now the only distinction between him and his superiors. Thus all distinction ceased, and every rank became, in a manner, upon an equality. Nor was this the end of the mischief; for a contest of such a nature amongst our servants necessarily destroyed all proportion between their wants and the honest means of satisfying them. In a country *where money is plenty, where fear is the principle of government, and where your arms are ever victorious, it is no wonder that the lust of riches should readily embrace the proffered means of its gratification, or that the instruments of your power should avail themselves of their authority, and proceed even to extortion in those cases where simple corruption could not keep pace with their rapacity*. Examples of this sort, set by superiors, could not fail being followed, in a proportionate degree, by inferiors. The evil was contagious, and spread among the civil and military, down to the writer, the ensign, and the free merchant."—Clive's Letter tc the Directors, Third Report of Parliamentary Committee, 1772.

The Directors replied to this very letter, lamenting their conviction of its literal truth:—"We have the strongest sense of the deplorable state to which our affairs were on the point of being reduced, from the corruption and rapacity of our servants, and *the universal depravity of manners throughout the settlement.* The general relaxation of all discipline and obedience, both military and civil, was hastily tending to a dissolution of all government. Our letter to the Select Committee expresses our sentiments of what has been obtained by way of donations; and to that we must add, that we think the vast fortunes acquired in the inland trade *have been obtained by a scene of the most tyrannic and oppressive conduct that was ever known in any age or country!*"

But however the Directors at home might lament, they were too far off to put an end to this "scene of the most tyrannic and oppressive conduct that was ever known in any age or country." This very same grave and eloquent preacher on this oppression and corruption, Clive, was the first to set the example of contempt of the Directors' orders, and condemnation of those evil practices. The Directors had sent out fresh covenants to be entered into by all their servants, both civil and military, binding them not to receive presents, nor to engage in inland trade; but it was found that the governor had not so much as brought the new covenants under the consideration of the council. The receipt of presents, and the inland trade by the Company's servants went on with increased activity. When at length these covenants were forwarded to the different factories and garrisons, General Carnac, and everybody else signed them. General Carnac however delayed his signing of them till he had time to obtain a present of two lacs of rupees (upwards of 20,000*l.*) from the reduced and impoverished Emperor. Clive appointed a committee to inquire into these matters, which brought to light strange scenes of rapacity, and of "threats to extort gifts." But what did Clive? He himself entered largely into private trade and into a vast monopoly of salt, an article of the most urgent necessity to the people; and this on the avowed ground of wishing some gentlemen whom he had brought out to make a fortune. His committee sanctioned the private trade in salt, betel-nut, and tobacco, out of which nearly all the abuses and miseries he complained of had grown, only confining it to the *superior servants* of the Company: and he himself, when the orders of the Directors were laid before him in council, carelessly turned them aside, saying, the Directors, when they wrote them, could not know what changes had taken place in India. No! they did not know that he and his council were now partners in the salt trade, and realizing a profit, including interest, of upwards of fifty per cent.! Perhaps Clive thought he had done a great service when he had attempted to lessen the number of harpies by cutting off the trading of the juniors, and thus turning the tide of gain more completely into his own pockets, and those of his fellows of the council. It must have been a very provoking sight to one with a development of acquistiveness so ample as his own, to witness what Verelst, in his "View of Bengal," describes as then existing. "At this time many black merchants found it expedient to purchase the name of any young writer in the Company's service by loans of money, and under this sanction harassed and oppressed the natives. So plentiful a supply was derived from this source, that many young writers were enabled to spend 1500*l.* and 2000*l.* per annum, were clothed in fine linen, and fared sumptuously every day." What were the miseries and insolent oppressions under which the millions of Bengal were made to groan by such practices, and by the lawless violence with which the revenues were collected about that period by the English, may be sufficiently indicated by the following passages. Mr. Hastings, in a letter to the President Vansittart, dated Bauglepore, April 25th, 1762, says—"I beg to lay before you a grievance which loudly calls for redress, and will, unless duly attended to, render ineffectual any endeavour to create a firm and lasting harmony between the Nabobs and the Company: I mean the oppressions committed under the sanction of the English name, and through the want of spirit to oppose them. The evil, I am well assured, is not confined to our dependents alone, *but is practised all over the country, by people falsely assuming the habit of our sepoys, or calling themselves our gomastahs.* On such occasions, the great power of the English intimidates the people from making any resistance; so, on the other hand, the indolence of the Bengalees, or the difficulty of gaining access to those who might do them justice, prevents our having knowledge of the oppressions. I have been surprised to meet with several English flags flying in places which I have passed; and on the river I do not believe I passed a boat without one. By whatever title they have been assumed, I am sure their frequency can boast no good to the Nabob's revenues, the quiet of the country, or the honour of our nation. A party of sepoys, who were on the march before us, afforded sufficient proofs of the rapacious and insolent spirit of these people when they are left to their own discretion. Many complaints against them were made to us on the road; *and most of the petty towns and serais were deserted at our approach, and the shops shut up, from the apprehension of the same treatment from us.*"

Mr. Vansittart endeavoured zealously to put a stop to such abominable practices; but what could he do? The very members of the council were deriving vast emoluments from this state of things, and audaciously denied its existence. Under such sanction, every inferior plunderer set at defiance the orders of the president and the authority of the officers appointed to prevent the commission of such oppressions on the natives. The native collectors of the revenue, when they attempted to levy, under the express sanction of the governor, the usual duties on the English, were not only repelled by them, but seized and punished as enemies of the

Company and violaters of its privileges. The native judges and magistrates were resisted in the discharge of their duties; and even their functions usurped. Everything was in confusion, and many of the zemindars and other collectors refused to be answerable for the revenues. Even the nabob's own officers were refused the liberty to make purchases on his own account. One of them, of high connexions and influence, was seized for having purchased from the nabob some saltpetre; the trade in which they claimed as belonging exclusively to them. He was put in irons and sent to Calcutta, where some of the council voted for having him publicly whipped, others desired that his ears might be cut off, and it was all that the president could effect to get him sent back to his own master to be punished. In Mr. Vansittart's own narrative is given a letter from one officer to the nabob, complaining that though he was furnished with instructions to send away Europeans who were found committing disorders to Calcutta, notwithstanding any pretence they shall make for so doing, he had used persuasions, and conciliated, and found them of no avail. That he had then striven by gentle means to stop their violences; upon which he was threatened that if he interfered with them or their servants, they would treat him in such a manner as should cause him to repent. That all their servants had boasted publicly, that this was what would be done to him did he presume to meddle. He adds, "Now, sir, I am to inform you what I obstructed them in. *This place (Backergunge) was of great trade formerly, but now brought to nothing by the following practices.* A gentleman sends a gomastah here to buy or sell. He immediately looks upon himself as sufficient to force every inhabitant either to buy his goods, or to force them to sell him theirs; and on refusal, or non-capacity, a flogging or confinement immediately ensues. This is not sufficient even when willing; but a second force is made use of, which is, to engross the different branches of trade to themselves, and not to suffer any persons to buy or sell the articles they trade in. They compel the people to buy or sell at just what rate they please, and my interfering occasions an immediate complaint. These, *and many other oppressions which are daily practised,* are the reasons that this place is growing destitute of inhabitants. . . . Before, justice was given in the public cutcheree, but now every gomastah is become a judge; they even pass sentence on the zemindars themselves; and draw money from them for pretended injuries."

Such was the state of the country in 1762, as witnessed by Mr. Hastings, and such it continued till Clive's government,—Clive, who so forcibly described it to the Directors; and what did Clive do? He aggravated it, enriched himself enormously by the very system, and so left it. Such it continued till Mr. Hastings,—this Mr. Hastings, who so feelingly had written his views and abhorrence of it to President Vansittart, came into supreme power; and what did the wise and benevolent Mr. Hastings? He became the Aaron's-rod of gift-takers; the prince of exactors, and the most unrelenting oppressor of the natives that ever visited India, or perhaps any other country. In the meantime this system of rapacity and extortion had reduced the people to the most deplorable condition of poverty and wretchedness imaginable. The monopoly of trade, and the violent abduction of all their produce in the shape of taxes, disspirited them to the most extreme degree, and brought on the country those famines and diseases for which that period is so celebrated. In 1770 occurred that dreadful famine, which has throughout Europe excited so much horror of the English. They have been accused of having directly created it, by buying up all the rice, and refusing to sell any of it except at the most exorbitant price. The author of the "Short History of the English Transactions in the East Indies," thus boldly states the fact. Speaking of the monopoly just alluded to, of salt, betel-nut, and tobacco, he says, "Money in this current came but by drops. It could not quench the thirst of those who waited in India to receive it. An expedient, such as it was, remained to quicken it. The natives could live with little salt, but could not want food. Some of the agents saw themselves well situated for collecting the rice into stores; they did so. They knew that the Gentoos would rather die than violate the principles of their religion by eating flesh. The alternative would therefore be between *giving what they had*, or *dying!* The inhabitants sunk. They that cultivated the land, and saw the harvest at the disposal of others, planted in doubt; scarcity ensued. Then the monopoly was easier managed,—sickness ensued. In some districts, the languid living left the bodies of their numerous dead unburied."—p. 145.

Many and ingenious have been the attempts to remove this awful opprobrium from our national character. It has been contended that famines are, or were of frequent occurrence in India;—that the natives had no providence; and that to charge the English with the miserable consequences of this famine is unreasonable, because it was what they could neither foresee nor prevent. Of the regular drought in the previous autumn there is no doubt; but there is unhappily as little, that the rapacity of the English had reduced the natives to that condition of poverty, apathy, and despair, in which the slightest derangement of season must superinduce famine;—that they were grown callous to the sufferings of their victims, and were as alive to their gain by the rising price through the scarcity, as they were in all other cases. Their object was sudden wealth; and they cared not, in fact, whether the natives lived or died, so that that object was effected. This is the relation of the Abbé Raynal, a foreign historian, and the light in which this event was beheld by foreign nations.

"It was by a drought in 1769, at the season when the rains are expected, that there was a failure of the great harvest of 1769, and the less harvest of 1770. It is true that the rice on the higher grounds did not suffer greatly by this disturbance of the seasons, but there was far from a sufficient quantity for the nourishment of all the inhabitants of the country; add to which the English, who were engaged beforehand to take proper care of their subsistence, as well as of the sepoys belonging to them, did not fail to keep locked up in their magazines a part of the grain, though the harvest was insufficient. . . . . This scourge did not fail to make itself felt throughout Bengal. Rice, which is commonly sold for one sol (½*d.*) for three pounds, was gradually raised so high as four or even six sols (3*d.*) for one pound; neither, indeed, was there any to be found, except in such places where the Europeans had taken care to collect it for their own use.

"The unhappy Indians were perishing every day by thousands under this want of sustenance, without any means of help and without any revenue. They were to be seen in their villages; along the public ways; in the midst of our European colonies,—pale, meagre, emaciated, fainting, consumed by famine—some stretched on the ground in expectation of dying; others scarce able to drag themselves on to seek any nourishment, and throwing themselves at the feet of the Europeans, entreating them to take them in as their slaves.

"To this description, which makes humanity shudder, let us add other objects, equally shocking. Let imagination enlarge upon them, if possible. Let us represent to ourselves, infants deserted, some expiring on the breasts of their mothers; everywhere, the dying and the dead mingled together; on all sides, the groans of sorrow and the tears of despair; and we shall then have some faint idea of the horrible spectacle which Bengal presented for the space of six weeks.

"During this whole time, the Ganges was covered with carcasses; the fields and highways were choked up with them; infectious vapours filled the air, and diseases multiplied; and one evil succeeding another, it appeared not improbable that the plague would carry off the total population of that unfortunate kingdom. It appears, by calculations pretty generally acknowledged, that the famine carried off a fourth part, that is to say—*about three millions!* What is still more remarkable, is, that such a multitude of human creatures, amidst this terrible distress, remained in absolute inactivity. All the Europeans, especially the English, were possessed of magazines. These were not touched. Private houses were so too. No revolt, no massacre, not the least violence prevailed. The unhappy Indians, resigned to despair, confined themselves to the request of succours they did not obtain; and peacefully awaided the relief of death.

"Let us now represent to ourselves any part of Europe afflicted with a similar calamity. What disorder! what fury! what atrocious acts! what crimes would ensue! How should we have seen amongst us Europeans, some contending for their food, dagger in hand, some pursuing, some flying, and without remorse massacring one another! How should we have seen men at last turn their rage on themselves; tearing and devouring their own limbs; and, in the blindness of despair, trampling under foot all authority, as well as every sentiment of nature and reason!

"Had it been the fate of the English to have had the like events to dread on the part of the people of Bengal, perhaps the famine would have been less general and less destructive. For, setting aside, as perhaps we ought, every charge of monopoly, no one will undertake to defend them against the reproach of negligence and insensibility. And in what a crisis have they merited that reproach? In the very instant of time in which the life or death of several millions of their fellow-creatures was in their power. One would think that in such alternative, the very love of humankind, that sentiment innate in all hearts, might have inspired them with resources." —i. 460-4.

CHAPTER III.

TREATMENT OF THE NATIVES—CONTINUED.

"If," says the same historian, in whose language we concluded the last chapter, "to this picture of public oppressions we were to add that of private extortions, we should find the agents of the Company almost everywhere exacting their tribute with extreme rigour, and raising contributions with the utmost cruelty. We should see them carrying a kind of inquisition into every family, and sitting in judgment on every fortune; robbing indiscriminately the artisan and the labourer; imputing it often to a man, as a crime, that he is not sufficiently rich, and punishing him accordingly. We should view them selling their favour and their credit, as well to oppress the innocent as to oppress the guilty. We should find, in consequence of these irregularities, despair seizing every heart, and an universal dejection getting the better of every mind, and uniting to put a stop to the progress and activity of commerce, agriculture, and population." This, which is the language of a foreigner, was also the language of the Directors at the same period, addressed to their servants in India. They complained that their "orders had been disregarded; that oppression pervaded the whole country; that youths had been suffered with impunity to exercise sovereign jurisdiction over the natives, and to acquire rapid fortunes by monopolizing commerce." They ask "whether there be a thing which had not been made a monopoly of? whether the natives are not more than ever oppressed and wretched?" They were just then appointing Mr. Hastings their first Governor-general, and expressed a hope that he would "set an example of temperance, economy, and application." Unfortunately Mr. Hastings set an example of a very different kind. It was almost immediately after his appointment to his high station that he entered into that infamous bargain with the Nabob of Oude for the extermination of the Rohillas; and during his government scarcely a year passed without the most serious charges being preferred against him to the supreme council, of which he himself was the head, of his reception of presents and annuities contrary to the express injunctions of the Company, and for the purpose of corrupt appointments. In 1775 he was charged with the receipt of 15,000 rupees, as a bribe for the appointment of the Duan of Burdwan, or manager of the revenues; in 1776, of receiving an annual salary from the Phousdar of Hoogly of 36,000 rupees, for a similar cause. About the same time it came out too, that in 1772, that is, immediately on entering the governorship, he received from the Munny Begum a present of one lac and a half of rupees, for appointing her the guardian and superintendent of the affairs of the Nabob of Bengal, a minor; and the same sum had been received by Mr. Middleton, his agent. The council felt itself bound to receive evidence on these charges. The Maha Rajah Nundcomar, who had been appointed to various important offices by Mr. Hastings himself, came forward and accused the governor of acquitting Mahmud Reza Khan, the Naib Duan of Bengal, and Rajah Shitabroy, the Naib Duan of Bahar, of vast embezzlements in their accounts, and also offered proof of the bribe of upwards of three and a half lacs from Munny Begum and Rajah Gourdass. What answer did he make to these charges? He refused to enter into them; but immediately commenced a prosecution of Nundcomar, on a charge of conspiracy; which failing, he had him tried on a charge of forgery, said to be committed five years before. On this he was convicted by a jury of Englishmen, and hanged, though the crime was not capital by the laws of his country. This was a circumstance that cast the foulest suspicions upon him. It was said that a man standing in the position and peculiar circumstances of the governor, accused of the high crimes of bribery and corruption, would, had he been innocent, have used every exertion to have saved the life of an accuser, had he been prosecuted by others, instead of himself hastening him out of the way; which must leave the irresistible conviction in the public mind, of his own guilt. But on the celebrated trial of Mr. Hastings, this was exactly the mode in which every accusation was met. When the most celebrated men of the time had united to reiterate these and other charges; when he stood before the House of Peers, impeached by the Commons, instead of standing forward as a man conscious of his innocence, and glad of the opportunity to clear his name from such foul taint, every technical obstruction which the ingenuity of his council could devise was thrown in the way of evidence. When the evidence of this Rajah Nundcomar, as taken by the supreme council of Calcutta, was tended, it was rejected because it was not given in the council upon oath; though Mr. Hastings well knew that the Hindoos never gave evidence upon oath, being contrary to their religion; that it was never required,—that this very evidence had been received by the council as legal; and that he himself had always contended during his own government, that such evidence was legal. When a letter of Munny Begum was presented, proving the reception of her bribe by Mr. Hastings, that letter was not admitted because it was merely a copy, though an attested one; the original letter itself was however produced, and persons high in office in India at the time of the transaction, came forward to swear to the hand and seal as those of the Begum. And what then? the original letter itself was rejected because it made part of the evidence before the council, which had been rejected before on other grounds!

Such was the manner in which these and the other great charges against this celebrated governor, which we have noticed in a former chapter, were met. Every piece of decisive evidence against him was resisted by every possible means: so that had he been the most innocent man alive, the only conviction that could remain on the mind of the public must have been that of his guilt. He had neither acted like an innocent, high-minded man, to whom the imputation of guilt is intolerable, himself in India, nor had his advocates in England been instructed to do so. Evidence on every charge, of the most conclusive nature, was offered, and resolutely rejected; and, spite of all the endeavours to clear the memory of Warren Hastings of cruelty and corruption, the very conduct of himself and his counsel on the trial, must stamp the accusing verdict indelibly on his name.

But his individual conduct is here of no further concern than to shew what must have been the contagion of his example, and what the license given by the House of Peers, by the rejection of evidence in such a case, to all future adventurers in India. Well might Burke exclaim, "That it held out to all future governors of Bengal the most certain and unbounded impunity. Peculation in India would be no longer practised, as it used to be, with caution and with secresy. It would in future stalk abroad at noon-day, and act without disguise; because, after such a decision as had just been made by their lordships, there was no possibility of bringing into a court the proofs of peculation." And indeed every misery which the combined evils of war, official plunder, and remorseless exaction could heap upon the unhappy natives, seems to have reigned triumphant through the British provinces and dependencies of India at this period. The destructive contests with Hyder Ali, the ravages of the English and their ally, the Nabob of Arcot, in Tanjore and the Marawars, were necessarily productive of extreme ruin and misery. During Mr. Hastings' government the duannee, or management of the revenues was assumed in Bengal by the English. Reforms both in the mode of collecting the taxes and in the administration of justice were attempted.

The lands were offered on leases of five years, and these leases put up to auction to the best bidders. The British Parliament in 1773 appointed a Supreme Court of Judicature, in which English judges administered English law. But as the great end aimed at was not the relief of the people, but the increase of the amount of taxation, these changes were only disastrous to the natives. Native officers were in many cases removed, and the native ryots only the more oppressed. Every change, in fact, seemed to be tried, except the simple and satisfactory one of reducing the exactions and cultivating the blessings of peace. Ten years after these changes had been introduced, and had been all this time inflicting unspeakable calamities on the people, Mr. Dundas moved inquiry into Indian affairs, and pronounced the most severe censures on both the Indian Presidencies and the Court of Directors. He accused the Presidencies, and that most justly, of plunging the nation into wars for the sake of conquest, of contemning and violating treaties, and plundering and oppressing the people of India. The Directors he charged with blaming the misconduct of their servants only when it was unattended with profit, and exercising a very constant forbearance as often as it was productive of gain or territory.

Of the effects of his own military and financial changes Mr. Hastings had a good specimen in his journey through the province of Benares in 1784. This was only three years after he had committed the atrocities in this province, related in a former chapter, and driven the Rajah from his throne; and these are his own words, in a letter to the Council, dated Lucknow, April, 1784:—"From the confines of Buxar to Benares, I was followed and fatigued by the clamours of the discontented inhabitants. The distresses which were produced by the long-continued drought unavoidably tended to heighten the general discontent: yet I have reason to fear that the cause principally existed in a defective, if not a corrupt and oppressive administration. From Buxar to the opposite boundary I have seen nothing but traces of complete devastation in every village." And what had occasioned those devastations? The wars and the determined resolve introduced by Mr. Hastings himself, to have the very uttermost amount that could be wrung from the people.

For the sort of persons to whom Mr. Hastings was in the habit of farming out the revenues of the provinces, and the motives for which they were appointed, we must refer to particulars which came out on his trial respecting such men as Kelleram, Govind Sing, and Deby Sing; but nothing can give a more lively idea of the horrid treatment which awaited the poor natives under such monsters as these collectors, than the statements then made of the practices of the last-mentioned person, Deby or Devi Sing. This man was declared to have been placed on his post for corrupt ends. He was a man of the most infamous character; yet that did not prevent Mr. Hastings placing him in such a responsible office, though he himself declared on the trial that he "so well knew the character and abilities of Rajah Deby Sing, that he could easily conceive it was in his power both to commit great enormities and to conceal the real grounds of them from the British collectors in the district."—Well, notwithstanding this opinion, the Rajah offered a very convenient sum of money, four lacs of rupees—upwards of 40,000*l.*—and he was appointed renter of the district of Dinagepore. Complaints of his cruelties were not long in arriving at Calcutta. Mr. Patterson, a gentleman in the Company's service, was sent as a commissioner to inquire into the charges against him; and the account of them, as given by Mr. Patterson, is thus quoted by Mills, from "The History of the Trial of Warren Hastings, Esq."

"The poor ryots, or husbandmen, were treated in a manner that would never gain belief if it was not attested by the records of the Company: and Mr. Burke thought it necessary to apologize to their lordships for the horrid relation with which he would be obliged to harrow their feelings. The worthy Commissioner Patterson, who had authenticated the particulars of this relation, had wished, that for the credit of human nature, he might have drawn a veil over them; but as he had been sent to inquire into them, he must, in the discharge of his duty, state those particulars, however shocking they were to his feelings. The cattle and corn of the husbandmen were sold for a third of their value, and their huts reduced to ashes! The unfortunate owners were obliged to borrow from usurers, that they might discharge their bonds, which had unjustly and illegally been extorted from them while they were in confinement; and such was the determination of the infernal fiend, Devi Sing, to have these bonds discharged, that the wretched husbandmen were obliged to borrow money, not at twenty, or thirty, or forty, or fifty, but at SIX HUNDRED per cent. to satisfy him! Those who could not raise the money were most cruelly tortured. *Cords were drawn tight round their fingers, till the flesh of the four on each hand was actually incorporated, and became one solid mass. The fingers were then separated again by wedges of iron and wood driven in between them!* Others were tied, two and two, by the feet, and thrown across a wooden bar, upon which they hung with their feet uppermost. They were then beat on the soles of the feet till the toe-nails dropped off! They were afterwards beat about the head till the blood gushed out at the mouth, nose, and ears. They were also flogged upon the naked body with bamboo canes, and prickly bushes, and above all, with some poisonous weeds, which were of a caustic nature, and burnt at every touch. The cruelty of the monster who had ordered all this, had contrived how to tear the mind as well as the body. He frequently had a father and son tied naked to one another by the feet and arms, and then flogged till the skin was torn from the flesh; and he had the devilish satisfaction to know, that every blow must hurt; for if one escaped the son, his sensibility was wounded by the knowledge he had, that the blow had fallen upon his father. The same torture was felt by the father, when he knew that every blow that missed him had fallen upon his son.

The treatment of the females could not be described. Dragged from the inmost recesses of their houses, which the religion of the country had made so many sanctuaries, they were exposed naked to public view. The virgins were carried to the Court of Justice, where they might naturally have looked for protection, but they now looked for it in vain; for in the face of the ministers of justice, in the face of the spectators, in the face of the sun, those tender and modest virgins were brutally violated. The only difference between their treatment and that of their mothers was, that the former were dishonoured in the face of day, the latter in the gloomy recesses of their dungeon. Other females had the nipples of their breasts put in a cleft bamboo, and torn off." What follows is too shocking and indecent to transcribe! It is almost impossible, in reading of these frightful and savage enormities, to believe that we are reading of a country under the British government, and that these unmanly deeds were perpetrated by British agents, and for the purpose of extorting the British revenue. Thus were these innocent and unhappy people treated, because Warren Hastings wanted money, and sold them to a wretch whom he knew to be a wretch, for a bribe; thus were they treated, because Devi Sing had paid his four lacs of rupees, and must wring them again out of the miserable ryots, though it were with their very life's blood, and with fire and torture before unheard of even in the long and black catalogue of human crimes. And it should never be forgotten, that though Mr. Burke pledged himself, if permitted, under the most awful imprecations, to prove every word of this barbarous recital, such permission was stoutly refused; and that, moreover, the evidence of the Commissioner Patterson stands in the Company's own records.

But it was not merely the commission of these outrages which the poor inhabitants had to endure. The English courts of justice, which should have protected them, became an additional means of torture and ruin. The writs of the supreme court were issued at the suit of individuals against the zemindars of the country in ordinary actions of debt. They were dragged from their families and affairs, with the frequent certainty of leaving them to disorder and ruin, any distance, even as great as 500 hundred miles, to give bail at Calcutta; a thing, which, if they were strangers, and the sum more than trifling, it was next to impossible they should have in their power. In default of this, they were consigned to prison for all the many months which the delays of English judicature might interpose between this calamitous stage and the termination of the suit. Upon the affidavit, into the truth of which no inquiry was made, upon the unquestioned affidavit of any person whatsoever—a person of credibility, or directly the reverse, no difference—the natives were seized, carried to Calcutta, and consigned to prison, where, even when it was afterwards determined that they were not within the jurisdiction of the court, and, of course, that they had been unjustly persecuted, they were liable to lie for several months, and whence they were dismissed totally without compensation. Instances occurred, in which defendants were brought from a distance to the Presidency, and when they declared their intention of pleading, that is, objecting to the jurisdiction of the court, the prosecution was dropped; but was again renewed; the defendant brought down to Calcutta, and again upon his offering to plead, the prosecution was dropped. The very act of being seized, was in India, the deepest disgrace, and so degraded a man of any rank that, under the Mahomedan government, it never was attempted but in cases of the utmost delinquency.—*Mills*.

In merely reading these cases of

> The proud man's contumely, the oppressor's wrong,

it is difficult to repress the burning indignation of one's

spirit. What shame, what disgrace, that under the laws of England, and in a country to which we owe so much wealth and power, such a system of reckless and desperate injustice should for a long series of years have been practising! But if it be difficult to read of it without curses and imprecations, what must it have been to bear? How must the wretched, hopeless, harassed, persecuted, and outraged people have called on Brahma for that tenth Avatar which should sweep their invincible, their iron-handed and iron-hearted oppressors, as a swarm of locusts from their fair land! Let any one imagine what must be the state of confusion when the zemindars, or higher collectors of the revenues, were thus plagued in the sphere of their arduous duties and called out of it, to the distant capital. When they were degraded in the eyes, and removed from the presence of the ryots, what must have been the natural consequence, but neglect and license on the part of the ryot, only too happy to obtain a little temporary ease? But the ryots themselves did not escape, as we have already seen. Such, however, continued this dismal state of things to the very end of the century. Lord Cornwallis complained in 1790, "that excepting the class of shroffs and banyans, who reside almost entirely in great towns, the inhabitants of these provinces were hastily advancing to a general state of poverty and wretchedness." Lord Cornwallis projected *his* plans, and in 1802, Sir Henry Strachey, in answer to interrogatories sent to the Indian judges, drew a gloomy picture of the result of all the schemes of finance and judicature that had been adopted. He represented that the zemindars, by the sale of their lands, in default of the payment of their stipulated revenue, were almost universally destroyed, or were reduced to the condition of the lowest ryots. That, in one year (1796) nearly one-tenth of all the lands in Bengal, Bahar, and Orissa, had been advertised for sale. That in two years alone, of the trial of the English courts, the accumulated causes threatened to arrest the course of justice: in one single district of Burdwan more than thirty thousand suits were before the judge; and that no candidate for justice could expect it in the course of an ordinary life. "The great men, formerly," said Sir Henry, "were the Mussulman rulers, whose places we have taken, and the Hindoo zemindars. These two classes are now ruined and destroyed." He adds, "exaction of revenue is now, I presume, and, perhaps, always was, the most prevailing crime throughout the country; and I know not how it is that extortioners appear to us in any other light than that of the worst and most pernicious species of robbers." He tells us that the lands of the Mahrattas in the neighbourhood of his district, Midnapore, were more prosperous than ours, though they were without regular courts of justice, or police. "Where," says he, "no battles are fought, the ryots remain unmolested by military exactions, and the zemindars are seldom changed, the country was in high cultivation, and the population frequently superior to our own."

Such was the condition and treatment of the natives of Hindostan, at the commencement of the present century. In another chapter, on our policy and conduct in this vast and important region—it remains only to take a rapid glance at the effect of these two centuries of despotism upon these subjected millions, and to inquire what we have since been doing towards a better state of things,—more auspicious to them, and honourable to ourselves.

CHAPTER IV.

TREATMENT OF THE NATIVES, CONTINUED—THEIR DEMORALIZATION.

We are accustomed to govern India—a country which God never gave us, by means which God will never justify.

Lord Erskine—Speech on Stockdale's Trial.

We have traced something of the misery which a long course of avarice and despotism has inflicted on the natives of India, but we have not taken into the account its moral effect upon them. Generation after generation of Englishmen flocked over to Hindostan, to gather a harvest of wealth, and to return and enjoy it at home. Generation after generation of Indians arose to create this wealth for their temporary visitors, and to sink deeper and deeper themselves into poverty. Happy had it been for them, had poverty and physical wretchedness come alone. But the inevitable concomitant of slavery and destitution appeared with them, and to every succeeding generation in a more appalling form—demoralization, vast as their multitude and dreadful as their condition. They were not more unhappy than they were degraded in spirit and debased in feeling. Ages of virtual though not nominal slavery, beneath Mahomedan and Christian masters, had necessarily done their usual work on the Hindus. They had long ceased to be the gentle, the pure-minded, the merciful Hindus. They had become cruel, thievish, murderous, licentious, as well as blindly superstitious. They had seen no religious purity, no moral integrity practised—how were they to become pure and honest? They had felt only cruelty and injustice—how were they to be anything but cruel and unjust? They had seen from age to age, from day to day, from hour to hour, every sacred tie of blood or honour, every moral obligation, every great and eternal principle of human action violated around them—how were they to reverence such things? How were they to regard them but as solemn and unprofitable mockeries? They were accordingly corrupted into a mean, lying, depraved, and perfidious generation—could the abject tools of a money-scraping race of conquerors be anything else?—was it probable? was it possible? Philosophers and poetical minds, when such, now and then, reached India, were astonished to find, instead of those delicate and spiritual children of Brahma, of whom they had read such delightful accounts—a people so sordid, and in many instances so savage and cruel. They had not calculated, as they might have done, the certain consequences of long years of slavery's most fatal inflictions. What an eternal debt of generous and Christian retribution do we owe India for all this! What, indeed, are the pangs we have occasioned, the poverty we have created, the evils of all kinds that we have perpetrated, to the moral degradation we have induced, and the gross darkness, gross superstition, the gross sensuality we have thus, in fact, fostered and perpetuated? Had we appeared in India as Christians instead of conquerors; as just merchants instead of subtle plotters, shunning the name of tyrants while we aimed at the most absolute tyranny; had we been as conspicuous for our diffusion of knowledge as for our keen, ceaseless, and insatiable gathering of coin; long ago that work would have been done which is but now beginning, and our power would have acquired the most profound stability in the affections and the knowledge of the people.

At the period of which I have been speaking—the end of the last and the opening of the present century, the character of the Hindus, as drawn by eye-witnesses of the highest authority, was most deplorable. Even Sir William Jones, than whom there never lived a man more enthusiastic in his admiration of the Hindu literature and antiquities, and none more ready to see all that concerned this people in sunny hues—even he, when he had had time to observe their character, was compelled to express his surprise and disappointment. He speaks of their cruelties with abhorrence: in his charge to the grand jury at Calcutta, June 10th, 1787, he observed, "Perjury seems to be committed by the meanest, and encouraged by some of the better sort of the Hindus and Mussulmans with as little remorse as if it were a proof of ingenuity, or even of merit"—that he had "no doubt that affidavits of any imaginary fact might be purchased in the markets of Calcutta as readily as any other article—and that, could the most binding form of religious obligation be hit upon, there would be found few consciences to bind."

All the travellers and historians of the time, Orme, Buchanan, Forster, Forbes, Scott, Waring, etc., unite in bearing testimony to their grossness, filth, and disregard of their words; their treachery, cowardice, and thievishness; their avarice, equal to that of the whites, and their cunning and duplicity more than European; their foul language and quarrelsome habits—all the features of a people depraved by hereditary oppression and moral neglect. Their horrid and barbarous superstitions, by which thousands of victims are destroyed every year, are now familiar to all Europe. Every particular of these evil lineaments of character were most strikingly attested by the Indian judges, in their answers to the circular of interrogatories put to them in 1801, already alluded to. They all coincided in describing the general moral character of the inhabitants as at the lowest pitch of infamy; that very few exceptions to that character were to be found; that there was no species of fraud or villany that the higher classes would not be guilty of; and that, in the lower classes, were to be added, murder, robbery, adultery, perjury, etc. etc., on the slightest occasion. One of them, the magistrate of Juanpore, added, "I have observed, among the inhabitants of this country, some possessed of abilities qualified to rise to eminence in other countries, *but a moral, virtuous man, I have never met amongst them.*"

Mr. Grant described the Bengalese as depraved and dishonest to a degree to which Europe could furnish no parallel; that they were "cunning, servile, intriguing, false, and hypocritically obsequious; that they, however, indemnified themselves for their passiveness to their superiors by their tyranny, cruelty, and violence to those in their power." Amongst themselves he says, "discord, hatred, abuse, slanders, injuries, complaints, and litigations prevail to a surprising degree. No stranger can sit down among them without being struck with the temper of malevolent contention and animosity as a prominent feature in the character of the society. It is seen in every village: the inhabitants live amongst each other in a sort of repulsive state. Nay, it enters into almost every family: seldom is there a household without its internal divisions and lasting enmities, most commonly, too, on the score of interest. The women, too, partake of this spirit of discord. Held in slavish subjection by the men, they rise in furious passions against each other, which vent themselves in such loud, virulent, and indecent railings, as are hardly to be heard in any other part of the world. . . . . . Benevolence has been represented as a leading principle in the minds of the Hindus; but those who make this assertion know little of their character. Though a Hindu would shrink with horror from the idea of directly slaying a cow, which is a sacred animal amongst them, yet he who drives one in his cart, galled and excoriated as she is by the yoke, beats her unmercifully from hour to hour, without any care or consideration of the consequence." Mr. Fraser Tytler, Lord Teignmouth, Sir James Mackintosh, and others, only expand the dark features of this melancholy picture; we need not therefore dwell largely upon it. The French missionary, the Abbé Dubois, and Mr. Ward, the English one, bear a like testimony. The latter, on the subject of Hindu humanity, asks—"Are these men and women, too, who drag their dying relations to the banks of rivers, at all seasons, day and night, and expose them to the heat and cold in the last agonies of death, without remorse;—who assist men to commit self-murder, encouraging them to swing with hooks in their backs, to pierce their tongues and sides—to cast themselves on naked knives or bury themselves alive—throw themselves in rivers, from precipices, and under the cars of their idols;—who murder their own children—burying them alive, throwing them to the alligators, or hanging them up alive in trees, for the ants and crows, before their own doors, or by sacrificing them to the Ganges;—who burn alive, amidst savage shouts, the heart-broken widow, by the hands of her own son, and with the corpse of a deceased father;—who every year butcher thousands of animals, at the call of superstition, covering themselves with blood, consigning their carcasses to the dogs, and carrying their heads in triumph through the streets,—are these the benignant Hindus?"

It may be said that these cruelties are the natural growth of their superstitions. True; but, up to the period in question, who had endeavoured to correct, or who cared for their superstitions so that they paid their taxes? To this hour, or, at least, till but yesterday, many of these bloody superstitions have had the actual sanction of the British countenance! To this hour the dreadful indications of their cruel and treacherous character, apart from their superstitions, from time to time affright Europe. We have latterly heard much of the horrible deeds of the Thugs and Phasingars. Where such dreadful associations and habits are prevalent to the extent described, there must be a most monstrous corruption of morals, shocking neglect of the people, and consequent annihilation of everything like social security and civilization. In what, indeed, does the practice and temper of the Thugs differ from those of the Decoits, who abounded at the period in question? These were gangs of robbers who associated for their purposes, and practised by subtle subterfuge or open violence, as best suited the occasion. They went in troops, and made a common assault on houses and property, or dispersed themselves under various disguises, to inveigle their victims into their power. Mr. Dowdeswell, in a report to government, in 1809, says, "robbery, rape, and murder itself, are not the worst figures in this horrid and disgusting picture. An expedient of common occurrence with the Decoits, merely to induce a confession of property supposed to be concealed, is to burn the proprietor with straws or torches until he discloses the property or perishes in the flames." He mentions one man who was convicted of having committed fifteen murders in nineteen days, and adds that, "volumes might be filled with the atrocities of the Decoits, every line of which would make the blood run cold with horror." He does, indeed, give some details of them of the most amazing and harrowing description.

Sir Henry Strachey, in his report already quoted, says, "the crime of decoity, in the district of Calcutta, has, I believe, greatly increased since the British administration of justice. The number of convicts confined at the six stations of this division (independent of Zillah twenty-four pergunnahs) is about 4000. Of them *probably nine-tenths are Decoits.* Besides these, some hundreds of late years have been transported. The number of persons convicted of decoity, however great it may appear, is certainly small in proportion to those who are guilty of the crime. At Midnapore I find, by the reports of the police darogars, that in the year 1802, a period of peace and tranquillity, they sent intelligence of no less than ninety-three robberies, most of them, as usual, committed by large gangs. With respect to fifty-one of these robberies, not a man was taken, and for the remaining forty-two, very few, frequently only one or two in each gang." Other judges describe the extent to which decoity existed, as being much vaster than was generally known, and calculated to excite the most general terror throughout the country.

This is an awful picture of a people approaching to one hundred millions, and of a great and splendid country, which has been for the most part in our hands for more than a century. It only remains now to inquire what has been done since the opening of the nineteenth century for the instruction and general amelioration of the condition of this vast multitude of human beings, and thereby for our own justification as a Christian nation. Warren Hastings said most truly, that throwing aside all pretences of any other kind that many were disposed to set up, the simple truth was, that "by the sword India had been acquired, and by the sword it must be maintained." If the forcible conquest of a country be, therefore, a crime against the rights of nations and the principles of religion, what retribution can we make for our national offences, except by employing our power to make the subjected people happy and virtuous? But if we do not hold even conquest to be a crime, or war to be unchristian, where is the man that will not deem that we have assumed an awful responsibility on the plainest principles of the Gospel, by taking into our hands the fate of so many millions of human creatures, thus degraded, thus ignorant and unhappy? It is impossible either to "do justice, to love mercy, or to walk humbly before God," without as zealously seeking the social and eternal benefit of so great a people, as we have sought, and still seek, our own advantage in the possession of their wealth. Over this important subject I am unfortunately bound to pass by my circumscribed limits, in a hasty manner. The subject would require a volume. It is with pleasure, however, that we can point to certain great features in the modern history of improvement in India. It is with pleasure that we can say that some of the most barbarous rites of the Hindu superstitions have been removed;

that infanticide and the burning of widows have been abolished by the British influençe; and that though the horrible immolations of Juggernaut are not terminated, they are no longer so unblushingly sanctioned, and even encouraged by British interference. These are great steps in the right path. To Colonel Walker, and Mr. Duncan the governor of Bombay, immortal thanks and honour are due, for first leading the way in this track of great reforms, by at once discouraging, dissuading from, and finally abolishing infanticide in Guzerat. One of the most beneficial acts of the Marquis Wellesley's government was to put this horrible custom down in Saugur. How little anything, however, but the extraction of revenue had throughout all the course of our dominion in India been regarded till the present century, the Christian Researches of Mr. Buchanan made manifest. The publication of that book, coming as it did from a gentleman most friendly to our authorities there, was the commencement of a new era in our Indian history. It at once turned, by the strangeness of its details, the eyes of the religious world on our Indian territories, and excited a feeling which more than any other cause has led to the changes which have hitherto been effected. At that period (1806), in making a tour through the peninsula of Hindostan, he discovered that everything like attention to the moral or religious condition of either natives or colonists was totally neglected. That all the atrocious superstitions of the Hindus were not merely tolerated, but even sanctioned, and some of them patronised by our government. That though there were above twenty English regiments in India at that time, *not one of them had a chaplain*, (p. 80). That in Ceylon, where the Dutch had once thirty-two Protestant churches, we had then but two English clergymen in the whole island! (p. 93). That there were in it by computation 500,000 natives professing Christianity, who, however, "had not one complete copy of the Scriptures in the vernacular tongue," and consequently they were fast receding into paganism (p. 95). That the very English were more notorious for their infidelity than anything else, and by their presence did infinite evil to the natives. That, in that very year, when the governor of Bombay announced to the supreme government at Calcutta, his determination to attempt to extirpate infanticide from Guzerat—a practice, be it remembered, which in that province alone, *destroyed annually* 3000 *children!* and it is said that infanticide, spite of the legal prohibition, is still privately perpetrated to a great extent in Cutch and Guzerat—this cool commercial body warned him "not even for the *speculative* success of that benevolent project, to hazard the *essential interests* of the state!" (p. 52). That all the horrors of burning widows were perpetrated to the amount of from seven hundred to *one thousand* of such diabolical scenes annually. That the disgusting and gory worship of Juggernaut was not merely practised, but was actually licensed and patronised by the English government. That very year it had imposed a tax on all pilgrims going to the temples in Orissa and Bengal; had appointed British officers, British gentlemen, to superintend the management of this hideous worship, and the receipt of its proceeds. That the internal rites of the temple consisted of one loathsome scene of prostitution, hired bands of women being kept for the purpose; its outward rites, the crushing of human victims under the car of the idol.

Thus the Indian government had, in fact, instead of discouraging such practices in the natives, taken up the trade of public murderers, and keepers of houses of ill fame, and that under the sacred name of religious tolerance! A more awful state of things it is impossible to conceive; nor one which more forcibly demonstrates what the whole of this history proclaims, that there is no state of crime, corruption, or villany, which by being familiarized to them, and coming to regard them as customary, educated men, and men of originally good hearts and pure consciences, will not eventually practise with composure, and even defend as right. What defences have we not heard in England of these very practices? It was not till recently that public opinion was able to put down the immolation of widows (1829), nor till this very moment that the Indian government has been shamed out of trading in murder and prostitution in the temples of Juggernaut. Thus, for more than thirty years has this infamous trade at Juggernaut been persisted in, from the startling exposure of it by Buchanan, and in the face of all the abhorrence and remonstrances of England—for more than a century and a half it has been tolerated. The plea on which it has been defended is that of delicacy towards the *opinions* of the natives. That delicacy, thus delicately extended where money was to be made, has not in a single case been practised for a single instant where our interest prompted a different conduct. We have seized on the lands of the natives; on their revenues; degraded their persons by the lash, or put them to death without any scruple. But this plea has been so strongly rebutted by one well acquainted with India, in the Oriental Herald, that before quitting this subject it will be well to quote it here. "The assumption that our empire is an empire of opinion in India, and that it would be endangered by restraining the bloody and abominable rites of the natives, is as false as the inference is unwarranted. Our empire is *not* an empire of opinion, it is not even an empire of law: it has been acquired; it is still governed; and can only be retained, unless the whole system of its government is altered, by the direct influence of force. No portion of the country has been voluntarily ceded, from the love borne to us by the original possessors. We were first permitted to land on the sea-coast to sell our wares, as humble and solicitous traders, till by degrees, sometimes by force, and sometimes by fraud, we have possessed ourselves of an extent of territory containing nearly a hundred millions of human beings. We have put down the ancient sovereigns of the land, we have stripped the nobles of all their power; and by continual drains on the industry and resources of the people, we take from them all their surplus and disposable wealth. There is not a single province of that country that we have ever acquired but by the direct influence which our strength and commanding power could enforce, or by the direct agency of warlike operations and superior skill in arms. There is not a spot throughout the whole of this vast region whereon we rule by any other medium than that by which we first gained our footing there—simple force. There is not a district in which the natives would not gladly see our places as rulers supplied by men of their own nation, faith, and manners, so that they might have a share in their own affairs; nor is there an individual out of all the millions subject to our rule in Asia, whose opinion is ever asked as to the policy or impolicy of any law or regulation about to be made by our government, however it may press on the interests of those subject to its operation. It is a delusion which can never be too frequently exposed, to believe that our empire in India is an empire of opinion, or to imagine that we have any security for our possession of that country, except the superiority of our means for maintaining the dominion of force."—vol. ii. p. 174.

CHAPTER V.

THE ENGLISH IN INDIA,—CONCLUDED.

THE preceding chapter is an awful subject of contemplation for a Christian nation. An empire over one hundred millions acquired by force, and held by force, for the appropriation of their revenues! Even this dominion of force is a fragile tenure. We even now watch the approaches of the gigantic power of Russia towards these regions with jealousy and alarm; and it is evident that at once security to ourselves, and atonement to the natives, are only to be found in the amelioration of their condition: in educating and Christianizing them, and in amalgamising them with British interests and British blood as much as possible. The throwing open of these vast regions, by the abolition of the Company's charter of trade, to the enterprise and residence of our countrymen, now offers us ample means of moral retribution; and it is with peculiar interest that we now turn to every symptom of a better state of things.

A new impulse is given to both commerce and agriculture. The march of improvement in the cultivation and manufacture of various productions is begun. The growth of wheat is encouraged, and even large quantities of fine flour imported thence into England. The indigo trade has become amazing, by the improvement in the manipulation of that article. Sugar, coffee, opium, cotton, spices, rice, every product of this rich and varied region, will all find a greater demand, and consequently a greater perfection from culture, under these circumstances. There is, in fact, no species of vegetable production which, in this glorious country, offering in one part or another the temperature of every known climate, may not be introduced. Such is the fertility of the land under good management, that the natives often now make 26*l.* per acre of their produce. The potato is becoming as much esteemed there as it has long been in Europe and America. Tea is likely to become one of its most important articles of native growth. Our missionaries of various denominations—episcopalians, catholics, baptists, methodists, moravians, etc., are zealously labouring to spread knowledge and Christianity; and there is nothing, according to the Christian brahmin, Rammohun Roy, which the Indian people so much desire as an English education. Let that be given, and the fetters of caste must be broken at once. The press, since the great struggle in which Mr. Buckingham was driven from India for attempting its freedom, has acquired a great degree of freedom. The natives are admitted to sit on petty juries; slavery is abolished;* and last, and best, education is now extensively and zealously promoted. The Company was bound by the terms of its charter in 1813 to devote 10,000*l.* annually to educating natives in the English language and English knowledge, which, though but a trifling sum compared with the vast population, aided by various private schools, must have produced very beneficial effects. Bishop Heber states that on his arrival in Bengal he found that there were fifty thousand scholars, chiefly under the care of Protestant missionaries. These are the means which must eventually make British rule that blessing which it ought to have been long ago. These are the means by which we may atone, and more than atone, for all our crimes and our selfishness in India. But let us remember that we are—after the despotism of two centuries, after oceans of blood shed by us, and oceans of wealth drained by us from India, and after that blind and callous system of exaction and European exclusion which has perpetuated all the ignorance and all the atrocities of Hindu superstition, and laid the burthen of them on our own shoulders—but at this moment on the mere threshold of this better career. Let us remember that still, at this hour, Hindostan is, in fact, the IRELAND OF THE EAST! It is a country pouring out wealth upon us, while it is swarming with a population of one hundred millions in the lowest state of poverty and wretchedness. It swarms with robbers and assassins of the most dreadful description: and it is impossible that it should be otherwise. It is said to be happy and contented under our rule; but such a happiness as its boldest advocates occasionally give us a glimpse of, may God soon remove from that oppressed country. Indeed, such are the features of it, even as drawn by its eulogists, as make us wonder that such wretchedness should exist under English sway. Our travellers describe the mass

* See note, p. 99.

of the labouring people as stunted in stature, especially the women; as half famished, and with hardly a rag to their backs. Mr. Tucker, himself a Director, and Deputy-Chairman of the Court of Directors, asks, "Whether it be possible for them to believe that a government, which seems disposed to appropriate a vast territory as *universal landlord*, and to collect, not *revenue*, but *rent*, can have any other view than to extract from the people the utmost portion which they can pay?" and adds, that "if the deadly hand of the tax-gatherer perpetually hover over the land, and threaten to grasp that which is not yet called into existence, its benumbing influence must be fatal, and the fruits of the earth will be stifled in the very germ."

Yet this is the constant system; and the poor ryots who cultivate farms of from six to twenty-four acres, but generally of the smaller kind, requiring only one plough, which, with other implements and a team of oxen, costs about 6*l*., are compelled to farm not such as they chose, but such as are alloted to them; to pay from one-half to two-thirds of their gross produce. If they attempt to run away from it, they are brought back and flogged, and forced to work. If after all, they cannot pay their quota, Sir Thomas Munro tells you, "*it must be assessed upon the rest.*" That where a crop *is even less than the seed*, the peasantry *should always be made to pay the full* rent where they can. And that all complaints on the part of the ryot, "should be listened to with very great caution." Is it any wonder that Hindostan is, and always has been full of robbers? Is this system not enough to make men run off, and do anything but work thus without hope; but it is not merely the work: look at the task-masters set over them. "A very large proportion of the talliars," says Sir Thomas Munro, "are themselves thieves; all the kawilgars are themselves robbers exempting them: and though they are now afraid to act openly, there is no doubt that many of them still secretly follow their former practices. Many potails and curnums also harbour thieves; so that no traveller can pass through the ceded districts without being robbed, who does not employ his own servants or those of the village to watch at night; and even this precaution is often ineffectual. Many offenders are taken, but great numbers also escape, for connivance must also be expected among the kawilgars and the talliars, who are themselves thieves; and the inhabitants are often backward in giving information from the fear of *assassination*." Colonel Stewart in 1825, asserted in his "Considerations on the Policy of the Government of India," that "if we look for absolute and bodily injury produced by our misgovernment, he did not believe that all the cruelties practised *in the lifetime* of the worst tyrant that ever sat upon a throne, even amounted to the quantity of human suffering inflicted by the Decoits *in one year* in Bengal." The prevalence of Thugs and Phasingars does not augur much improvement in this respect yet; nor do recent travellers induce us to believe that the picture of popular misery given us about half a dozen years ago by the author of "Reflections on the Present State of British India," is yet become untrue.

"Hitherto the poverty of the cultivating classes, men who have both property and employment, has been alone considered; but the extreme misery to which the immense mass of the unemployed population are reduced, would defy the most able pen adequately to describe, or the most fertile imagination to conceive. . . . . On many occasions of ceremony in families of wealthy individuals it is customary to distribute alms to the poor; sometimes four annas, about three-pence, and rarely more than eight annas each. When such an occurrence is made known, the poor assemble in astonishing numbers, and the roads are covered with them from twenty to fifty miles in every direction. On their approaching the place of gift, no notice is taken of them, though half famished, and almost unable to stand, till towards evening, when they are called into an inclosed space, and huddled together for the night, in such crowds, that notwithstanding their being in the open air, it is surprising how they escape suffocation. When the individual who makes the donation perceives that all the applicants are in the inclosure (by which process he guards against the possibility of any poor wretch receiving his bounty twice), he begins to dispense his alms, either in the night, or on the following morning, by taking the poor people, one by one, from the place of their confinement, and driving them off as soon as they have received their pittance. The number of people thus accumulated, generally amounts to from twenty to fifty thousand; and from the distance they travel, and the hardships they endure for so inconsiderable a bounty, some idea may be formed of the destitute condition.

"In the interior of Bengal there is a class of inhabitants who live by catching fish in the ditches and rivulets; the men employing themselves during the whole day, and the women travelling to the nearest city, often a distance of fifteen miles, to sell the produce. The rate at which these poor creatures perform their daily journey is almost incredible, and the sum realized is so small as scarcely to afford them the necessaries of life. In short, throughout the whole of the provinces the crowds of poor wretches who are destitute of the means of subsistence are beyond belief. On passing through the country, they are seen to pick the undigested grains of food from the dung of the elephants, horses, and camels; and if they can procure a little salt, large parties of them sally into the fields at night, and devour the green blades of corn or rice the instant they are seen to shoot above the surface. Such, indeed, is their wretchedness that they envy the lot of the convicts working in chains upon the roads, and have been known to incur the danger of criminal prosecution, in order to secure themselves from starving by the allowance made to those who are condemned to hard labour."

Such is the condition of these native millions, from

whose country our countrymen, flocking over there, according to the celebrated simile of Burke, "like birds of prey and of passage, to collect wealth, have returned with most splendid fortunes to England." What is the avowed slavery of some half million of negroes in the West Indies, who have excited so much interest amongst us, to the virtual slavery of these *hundred millions* of Hindus in their own land? It is declared that these poor creatures are happy under our government—but it should be recollected that so it has been, and is, said of the negroes; and it should be also recollected what Sir John Malcolm said, in 1824, in a debate at the India-house—himself a governor and a laudator of our system, that "even the instructed classes of natives have a hostile feeling towards us, which was not likely to decrease from the necessity they were under of concealing it. My attention," he said, "has been during the last five-and-twenty years particularly directed to this dangerous species of secret war carried on against our authority, which is *always carried on* by numerous though unseen hands. The spirit is kept up by letters, by exaggerated reports, and by pretended prophecies. When the time appears favourable from the occurrence of misfortune to our arms, from rebellion in our provinces, or from mutiny in our troops, circular letters and proclamations are dispersed over the country with a celerity that is incredible. *Such documents are read with avidity.* Their contents are in most cases the same. The English are depicted as *usurpers* of low caste, and as tyrants, who have sought India only to degrade them, to rob them of their wealth, and subvert their usages and religion. The native soldiers are always appealed to, and the advice to them is in all instances I have met with, the same,—'your European tyrants are few in number—*murder them!*'"

How far are these evils diminished since the last great political change in India—since the abolition of the Company's charter, and they became, not the commercial monopolists, but the governors of India? Dr.

Spry, of the Bengal Medical Staff, can answer that in his "Modern India," published in 1837. The worthy doctor describes himself as a short time ago (1833) being on an expedition to reduce some insurrectionary Coles in the provinces of Benares and Dinapore. "Next morning," he says, "Feb. 9th, we went out in three parties to burn and destroy villages! Good fun, burning villages!" The mode of expression would lead one to suppose that the doctor extremely enjoyed "the good fun of burning villages;" but the general spirit of his work being sensible and humane, we are bound to suppose that his expressions and his notes of admiration are ironical, and meant to indicate the abhorrence such acts deserves; for he immediately tells us that these Coles seemed very inoffensive sort of people, and laid down their arms in large numbers the moment they were invited to do so.

Dr. Spry tells us that the Anglo-Indian government, in 1836, had come to the admirable resolution to make the English language the vernacular tongue throughout Hindostan. That would be, in effect, to make it entirely an English land—to leaven it rapidly, and for ever, with the spirit, the laws, the literature, and the religion of England. It is impossible to make the English language the vernacular tongue, without at the same time producing the most astonishing moral revolution which ever yet was witnessed on the earth. English ideas, English tastes, English literature and religion, must follow as a matter of course. It is curious, indeed, already to hear of the instructed natives of Hindostan holding literary and philosophical meetings in English forms, debating questions of morals and polite letters, and adducing the opinions of Milton, Shakspeare, Newton, Locke, etc. Dr. Spry states that the Committee of Public Instruction are about to establish schools for educating the natives in English, at Patnah, Dacca, Hazeeribagh, Gohawati, and other places; and that the native princes in Nepaul, Manipúr, Rajpootanah, the Punjaub, etc. were receiving instructions in English, and desirous to promote it in their territories. This is most encouraging; but Dr. Spry gives us other facts of a less agreeable nature. From these we learn that the ancient canker of India, excessive and unremitting exaction, is at this moment eating into the very vitals of the country as actively as ever. He says that "it is in the territories of the independent native chiefs and princes that great and useful works are found and maintained. In our territories, the canals, bridges, reservoirs, wells, groves, temples, and caravansaries, the works of our predecessors, from revenues expressly appropriated to such undertakings, are going fast to decay, together with the feelings which originated them; and unless a new and more enlightened policy shall be followed, of which the dawn may, perhaps, be distinguished, will soon leave not a trace behind. A persistance for a short time longer in our selfish administration will level the face of the country, as it has levelled the ranks of society, and leave a plain surface for wiser statesmen to act on.

"At present, the aspect of society presents no middle class, and the aspect of the country is losing all those great works of ornament and utility with which we found it adorned. Great families are levelled, and lost in the crowd; and great cities have dwindled into farm villages. The work of destruction is still going on, and unless we act on new principles will proceed with desolating rapidity. How many thousand links by which the affections of the people are united to the soil, and to their government, are every year broken and destroyed by our selfishness and ignorance; and yet, if our views in the country extended beyond the returns of a single harvest, beyond the march of a single detachment, or the journey of a single day, we could not be so blind to their utility and advantage." He adds: "By our revenue management we have shaken the entire confidence of the rural population, who no longer lay out their little capital in village improvement, lest our revenue officers, at the expiration of their leases, should take advantage of their labours, and impose an additional rent. . . . . With regard to Hindostan, those natives who are unfriendly to us *might with justice declare our conduct to be more allied to Vandalism than to civilization*. . . . . . Burke's severe rebuke still holds good,—that if the English were driven from India, they would leave behind them no memorial worthy of a great and enlightened nation; no monument of art, science, or beneficence; no vestige of their having occupied and ruled over the country, except such traces as the vulture and the tiger leave behind them."—pp. 10-18. He tells us that a municipal tax was imposed under pretence of improving and beautifying the towns, but that the improvements very soon stopped, while the tax is still industriously collected. In the appendix to his first volume, we find detailed all the miseries of the ryots as we have just reviewed them; and he tells us that of this outraged class are *eleven-twelfths of the population!* and quotes the following sentence from 'The Friend of India,' "A proposal was some time since made, or rather a wish expressed, to domesticate the art of caricaturing in India. Here is a fine subject. The artist should first draw the lean and emaciated ryot, scratching the earth at the tail of a plough, drawn by two half-starved, bare-ribbed bullocks. Upon his back he would place the more robust Seputneedar, and upon his shoulders the Durputneedar; he again should sustain the well-fed Putneedar; and upon his shoulders should be represented to crown the scene, the big Zemindar, that compound of milk, sugar, and clarified butter. . . . The poor ryot pays for all! He is drained by these middle men; he is cheated by his banker out of twenty-four per cent. at least; and his condition is beyond description or imagination"

Dr. Spry attests the present continuance of those scenes of destitution and abject wretchedness to which I have but a few pages back alluded. He has seen the miserable creatures picking up the grains of corn from the soil of the roads. "I have seen," says he, "hundreds of the famishing poor, traversing the jungles of Bundlecund, searching for wild berries to satisfy the cravings of hunger. Many, worn down by exhaustion or disease, die by the road-side, while mothers, to preserve their offspring from starvation, sell or give them to any rich man they can meet!" He himself, in 1834, was offered by such a mother her daughter of six years old for fourteen shillings!—vol. i. 297.

These are the scenes and transactions in our great Indian empire—that splendid empire which has poured out such floods of wealth into this country; in which such princely presents of diamonds and gold have been heaped on our adventurers; from the gleanings of which so many happy families in England* "live at home at ease," and in the enjoyment of every earthly luxury and refinement. For every palace built by returned

* Even so recently as 1827 we find some tolerably regal instances of regal gifts to our Indian representatives. Lord and Lady Amherst on a tour in the provinces arrived at Agra. Lady Amherst received a visit from the wife of Hindoo Row and her ladies. They proceeded to invest Lady Amherst with the presents sent for her by the Byza Bhye. They put on her a turban richly adorned with the most costly diamonds, a superb diamond necklace, ear-rings, anklets, bracelets, and amulets of the same, valued at 30,000*l.* sterling. A complete set of gold ornaments, and another of silver, was then presented. Miss Amherst was next presented with a pearl necklace, valued at 5,000*l.*, and other ornaments of equal beauty and costliness. Other ladies had splendid presents—the whole value of the gifts amounting to 50,000*l.* sterling!

In the evening came Lord Amherst's turn. On visiting the Row, his hat was carried out and brought back on a tray covered. The Row uncovered it, and placed it on his lordship's head, overlaid with the most splendid diamonds. His lordship was then invested with other jewels to the reputed amount of 20,000*l.* sterling. Presents followed to the members of his suite. Lady Amherst took this opportunity of retiring to the tents of the Hindu ladies, *where presents were again given;* and a bag of 1000 rupees to her ladyship's female servants, and 500 rupees to her interpretess.

Oriental Herald, vol. xiv. p. 444.

Indian nabobs in England; for every investment by fortunate adventurers in India stock; for every cup of wine and delicious viand tasted by the families of Indian growth amongst us, how many of these Indians themselves are now picking berries in the wild jungles, sweltering at the thankless plough only to suffer fresh extortions, or snatching with the bony fingers of famine, the bloated grains from the manure of the highways of their native country!

I wonder whether the happy and fortunate—made happy and fortunate by the wealth of India, ever think of these things?—whether the idea ever comes across them in the luxurious carriage, or at the table crowded with the luxuries of all climates?—whether they glance in a sudden imagination from the silken splendour of their own abodes, to the hot highways and the pestilential jungles of India, and see those naked, squalid, famishing, and neglected creatures, thronging from vast distances to the rich man's dole, or feeding on the more loathsome dole of the roads? It is impossible that a more strange antithesis can be pointed out in human affairs. We turn from it with even a convulsive joy, to grasp at the prospects of education in that singular country. Let the people be educated, and they will soon cease to permit oppression. Let the English engage themselves in educating them, and they will soon feel all the sympathies of nature awaken in their hearts towards these unhappy natives. In the meantime these are all the features of a country suffering under the evils of a long and grievous thraldom. They are the growth of ages, and are not to be removed but by a zealous and unwearying course of atoning justice. Spite of all flattering representations to the contrary, the British public should keep its eye fixed steadily on India, assuring itself that a debt of vast retribution is there due from us; and that we have only to meet the desire now anxiously manifested by the natives *for education*, to enable us to expiate towards the children all the wrongs and degradations heaped for centuries on the fathers; and to fix our name, our laws, our language and religion, as widely and beneficently there as in the New World!

Though education is alluded to by the author of these chapters, as a great and necessary means of amending the condition of the natives of India, it is only one of many means which must be adopted and vigorously prosecuted, before any considerable amelioration can take place. The work of education is effectually retarded by the extreme poverty of the people, the parsimony and lethargy of the government, and the suspicion and discontent which are the natural results of the course which has been so long pursued. A deep and extensive reform in the revenue and fiscal systems of this country is imperatively demanded. The rights of the cultivators—now disregarded and trampled upon, must be recognized and respected. Those fearful visitations, in the shape of famines, which have so long and so frequently desolated the richest and most populous regions of India, must be averted, as they may be, by delivering the natives from that state of absolute poverty, which leaves them without the means of subsisting for a week, when the earth refuses to "yield her increase." When that flood of intelligence regarding the real state of British India, which we trust is at hand, is poured upon the public, it will be matter of astonishment and reproach, that, as a nation, we have been so long in utter ignorance of the claims of a hundred millions of our brethren, and of the immense and exhaustless value of that magnificent empire, which is the richest (and might be the brightest) jewel in the diadem of our sovereign. The intelligence referred to, will demonstrate also, that the cause of liberty and humanity all over the world, can be immeasurably advanced, by the commencement and zealous perseverance in a wise and benevolent course of policy towards our Eastern Possessions. India may be made the instrument of redeeming Africa, and regenerating America, as well as of enriching Great Britain, Allusion is here made to the boundless facilities which India presents, for the cultivation of those articles which are now the produce of slave labour. When the merchant, philanthropist, and abolitionist of this country, shall be brought to sit down together, to study the map of India, they will see that by a simple, certain, and easy process, they can put down the execrable traffic in human beings on the shores of Africa, and all the horrors of slavery in North and South America; and they will be filled with surprise at the mingled folly, infatuation, and crime, which have hitherto permitted to live, and helped to thrive,—the brutal, unjust, and murderous systems, which have stained the earth and the ocean with the blood of the helpless and the innocent.

Every friend of India, will rejoice to learn, that a Society is about to be formed, for improving the condition of our fellow subjects, the natives of the East; and that the first step which it is intended to take, is, to gather, from every authentic source, the most useful and valuable information upon every topic connected with the welfare of India, and to scatter that information over the face of the entire country. Such an institution has been long wanted, and never more than at the present moment. Such an institution, properly supported, and wisely conducted, may be one of the greatest blessings to India and the world at large. We know not the individual to whom the object of the proposed Society does not appeal. It appeals to the abolitionist, for in India there is slavery to be abolished,—to the friend of humanity, for in India there is an inconceivable mass of indigence and misery,—to the friend of education, for in India, millions are perishing for "lack of knowledge,"—to the friend of religion, for in India "gods many," of a false, polluting, and sanguinary character, have usurped the worship of the true God,—to the statesman, politician, and patriot; because in the history, government, condition, and prospects of India, there is every thing calculated to interest the mind of the man who is concerned for the fate of his own or other nations. A volume might be filled with evidence that India is, beyond every other part of the world, a field to allure the merchant, the manufacturer, the artisan, the shipowner, and the capitalist. What is before them when they look to India? A safe and certain passage—a vast and fertile country—a teeming and willing population—varied, costly, and marketable produce—a people whose wants might give employment to every starving and dissatisfied labourer in every part of Great Britain—a commerce between different portions of the British dominions, which may be carried on to an indefinite extent, and which, while it raises and relieves the myriads of the East, will occupy the hands and replenish the pockets of all classes in this country, and at the same time be rapidly dissolving the fetter of the slave, and starving from the shores of Africa and America, the miscreant man-thief who drives his horrid trade, under the commission furnished him (oh shame!) by Christian countries.

The preceding pages go forth wholly independent of any committee or society; but, as those at whose desire they are republished, feel a deep interest in the intended movement on behalf of British India, they think they cannot more appropriately conclude this little Work than by inserting the Prospectus which has been recently issued.

PROSPECTUS
OF
THE PROVISIONAL COMMITTEE,
FOR FORMING A
BRITISH INDIA SOCIETY,
FOR BETTERING THE CONDITION OF OUR FELLOW-SUBJECTS—THE NATIVES OF BRITISH INDIA.

Provisional Committee.
With power to add to their number.

ADAM, WILLIAM, ESQ., LATE OF CALCUTTA.
ALDAM, WILLIAM, JUN., ESQ., LEEDS.
BACKHOUSE, JONATHAN, ESQ., DARLINGTON.
BLAIR, W. THOMAS, ESQ., BATH.
BOWRING, JOHN, ESQ., LL.D.
BRIGGS, MAJOR-GENERAL.
BROUGHAM, LORD.
BROWN, F. C., ESQ., TELLICHERRY
CHRISTY, THOMAS, JUN., ESQ.
CLARKSON, THOMAS, ESQ.
FORBES, SIR CHARLES, BART.
FOSTER, VESEY LESLIE, ESQ.
HARDCASTLE, J. ALFRED, ESQ.
HARFORD, JAMES, ESQ., BRISTOL.
HARFORD, JOHN, ESQ., BRISTOL.
HOWITT, WILLIAM, ESQ.
PEASE, JOSEPH, SEN., ESQ., DARLINGTON.
SMITH, SIR CULLING EARDLEY, BART.
THOMPSON, GEORGE, ESQ.

Treasurer.
MAJOR-GENERAL BRIGGS, 11, YORK GATE, REGENT'S PARK.

Honorary Secretary.
F. C. BROWN, ESQ. 22, HARLEY STREET.

Travelling Secretary.
GEORGE THOMPSON, ESQ.

Bankers.
LONDON AND WESTMINSTER BANK, 9, WATERLOO PLACE, AND LOTHBURY.

Assistant Secretary.
MR. EDWARD BALDWIN.

TEMPORARY OFFICE, GUILDHALL COFFEE HOUSE, KING STREET, CHEAPSIDE, LONDON.

It is admitted in Great Britain, and known to be but too true by all who have had personal experience of the real state of India, that although a commercial intercourse has existed between the British Isles and India, for more than two hundred years, and the Government of this Empire now rules over a hundred millions of the inhabitants of the East, there is, nevertheless, a general want of information upon Indian affairs, and an almost total indifference felt respecting them. It must be obvious to all who reflect upon these facts, that such a state of things contrasts strangely with the duty we owe to our distant Dominions, with the extent, the value, and the importance of our East Indian Possessions, and with the many and vast Interests involved in the Question.

British India is an Empire as large as Europe (exclusive of Russia), with a population, including tributary States, of more than one hundred and fifty millions. Over this Empire and People, a sway is exercised wholly *British;* and consequently, the want of an accurate knowledge of Indian affairs, and the absence of a proper interest in the public at large for the welfare of the Natives, must operate prejudicially upon their minds, since they cannot but feel that their destinies are influenced by the disposition manifested towards them in the parent Country.

From the perusal of a variety of official and other Documents of recent date, it appears that ignorance, poverty, crime, and disaffection, prevail to a distressing and alarming extent throughout the British Indian Territories. It also appears, that during the last twenty years, though a period of profound peace, there has been a succession of Famines of the most desolating description. It has been estimated that the Famine of 1837—38, in the Upper Provinces of Bengal, swept off more than half a million of the inhabitants. Famines are this year ravaging the Northern Provinces of Bombay and Madras. These calamitous events are rendered the more mysterious and affecting, when viewed in connexion with the statement, that the soil of India is a soil of unequalled fertility, and that a very large portion of it (by some authorities, computed at one half) lies uncultivated, and covered with jungle, the haunts of wild beasts.

Information on these subjects has, within the last few months, been laid before the public in various parts of the Kingdom. The result has been, a deep feeling of compassion in the minds of many humane and influential persons, and the formation of Associations for promoting the welfare of the Natives of India, in Sheffield, Glasgow, Newcastle-upon-Tyne, Edinburgh, Darlington, etc. A strong desire has, besides, been expressed for the establishment of a Metropolitan Society for the same object; by whose inquiries and efforts, the friends of India, throughout Great Britain, might be guided and assisted in this new and benevolent undertaking.

In consequence of these circumstances, and in accordance also with their own deep feeling of interest in the subject, the individuals whose names are attached to this Prospectus, have, after mature deliberation, resolved themselves into a PROVISIONAL COMMITTEE, for forming a Society to be designated "THE BRITISH INDIA SOCIETY, for bettering the condition of our fellow-subjects—The Natives of British India.

In making known this resolution to the public, the Committee consider it their duty to state very briefly, but distinctly, their motives and plans.

The Committee has its origin in a regard for the welfare of the Natives of India, who, owing allegiance to the Government, are entitled to look for sympathy and succour from the people of England. The Committee desire to found the proposed Society upon the strictest principles of Justice and Humanity:—upon a basis which will permanently exclude the adoption of party, of sectarian, or mercenary views. They contemplate the use of those means only which are moral, peaceful, and constitutional. They would suggest, and labour to secure, the delay of all specific plans of amelioration, until every doubt respecting the nature and extent of alleged existing evils, and the necessity of remedying them, is entirely removed.

The primary duty of a BRITISH INDIA SOCIETY would therefore be,—to obtain from every available source, authentic and impartial information, respecting the present actual condition of the Natives of India, and the circumstances of the Country; and to give to the information so obtained, the widest possible circulation. The means of accomplishing this necessary preliminary object appear to be:—viz.

To bring together, analyse, condense, and diffuse, the facts already at hand.

To adopt the best means of obtaining regular and systematic information from all parts of India.

To begin a Collection of the most useful Works on every branch of the subject.

To issue, under proper management, a Periodical Publication, containing the most recent, important, and interesting Indian intelligence.

To reprint, in whole or in part, such Works as may be calculated to elucidate particular portions of the great subject.

To employ an active, experienced, and effective Agency, for the organization of Provincial Auxiliary Societies.

The judicious and zealous prosecution of a course, such as has been now described, would, the Committee feel assured, effectually remove the apathy which at present exists. That apathy, they believe, may with justice be ascribed to the difficulty which has hitherto attended the search after correct and comprehensive information, respecting the condition and character of the Natives of India, and the nature and effects of British rule in the East.

The Committee entertain no doubt, that, when the vast importance of our Eastern Possessions is understood—when the claims of one hundred millions of British Subjects are recognized and felt—and when the responsibility and moral obligation of this Nation towards them are considered, a great and generous effort will promptly be made, to benefit a Country, which contains within itself the means of returning a hundred-fold into the bosoms of its benefactors, all the blessings they can possibly confer upon it.

The Committee prefer to make their appeal to the just principles and Christian feelings of the Country. They are not ignorant, however, of the extent to which they might address themselves to the loyalty, the patriotism, and the interests of their fellow-citizens; but they believe that such an appeal is unnecessary. They feel convinced that no argument is required to demonstrate the inseparable connexion between the bettering of the social, moral, and intellectual condition of the countless millions of India, and the accomplishment of those ends which are sought by the promoters and patrons of legitimate commerce, and the advocates of the honour, the stability, and the prosperity of the British Empire, at home and abroad.

The Committee having stated the objects, principles, and plans, according to which they are about to attempt the formation of a British India Society, look with confidence for the sanction, support, and co-operation of the British public. They sincerely and earnestly solicit advice. They especially desire the aid of Gentlemen who have resided in India, and who, after perusing this Prospectus, feel that they can cordially unite in the work proposed.

Finally, the Committee respectfully solicit pecuniary assistance. Subscriptions and Donations will be gratefully received by the Treasurer, Secretaries, Bankers, and Members of the Committee.

May 24th, 1839.

*** It is the intention of the Provisional Committee to give due notice of the public formation of the proposed Society, and to invite the presence and aid, on the occasion, of those Friends, in different parts of the Kingdom, who may have already espoused the Cause, or who may be desirous of doing so.

P.S.—Since the first Edition of this Prospectus was issued, the Committee have received, from various parts of the Country the most encouraging assurances of sympathy and support. The Committee have been peculiarly gratified by the Resolution passed at the Annual Meeting of the Relief Synod of Scotland, on the 14th inst.—recognising the great importance of the object the Committee have in view, and pledging the co-operation of that respectable and influential body. The friends of humanity will rejoice to find that THOMAS CLARKSON, Esq., the venerable and enlightened Friend of African freedom, has heartily united with those who are associated in this effort for the improvement of the condition of their fellow-subjects, the Natives of British India.

Note.—On page 82, it is stated that slavery is abolished. This unhappily is not the fact. Slavery still exists to a great extent in British India. It was the intention of the original framers of the Bill of 1833, for renewing the East India Company's Charter, to put an end to Slavery throughout the whole of British India, and accordingly, a clause was inserted to that effect.

During the progress of the Bill, however, through the House of Lords, a clause was substituted, instructing the Governor General in Council to take into consideration the means of *mitigating* the State of Slavery, and of ameliorating the condition of Slaves, and of extinguishing Slavery throughout the British Territories, so soon as such extinction shall be practicable and safe.

Nothing effectual, up to the present time, has been done to put an end to slavery in India. We understand the Government at Calcutta have called for returns upon the subject, with a view to the adoption of ulterior measures.

APPENDIX.

Exports and Imports.

The following table is submitted for the purpose of exhibiting the very remarkable difference between the Imports and Exports of British India, and those of other parts of the world. It will be seen that the first four places named (British colonies) are identical in no one point besides *the tenure of land*, which is in all, as in England, *private property*. In *British India*, the East India Company, in trust for the people of England, *assume to be the* SOLE PROPRIETORS OF THE SOIL.* This fact will, it is believed, to a very great extent, account for the striking disparity which appears. No opportunity is afforded in this place, of going into the minute and peculiar circumstances of the populations referred to below; but granting that, in some cases, these may be sufficient to account in part for the extraordinary disproportion which appears, there will still remain enough to challenge investigation, and afford *prima facie* evidence of gross and ruinous misgovernment. In Mauritius we find a population of ninety thousand souls, exporting to Great Britain to the amount of 697,000*l.* sterling; while the exports from British India, with a population of *one hundred million*, amount only to *two millions and a half*. Again, while the taxes paid in Mauritius are equal to 2*l.* 12*s.* 8*d.* per head, the taxation in India, though enough to impoverish, and often to bring to utter ruin the inhabitants, amounts to but 5*s.* 9*d.* per head.

Colony.	Square Miles.	Population.	Imports from Great Britain.	Exports to Great Britain.	Laws and Language.	Tenure of Land.	Taxation per Head.
MAURITIUS (1837). .	676	90,000	356,000	697,000	French.	Private Property	£ s. d. 2 12 8
Sydney, or E. Australia	50,000	85,000	794,000	514,000	English.	Ditto.	3 17 7
British Guiana . . .	100,000	99,710	666,000	1,929,000	Dutch.	Ditto.	1 11 3
Trinidad .	2,400	39,045	233,000	298,000	Spanish.	Ditto.	1 3 0
British India	500,000	100,000,000	3,440,000	2,500,000	Various.	The East India Company the Landlord.	0 5 9

* "Virtually, it is true, the British Government has made itself proprietor of the land; it is by this authority taxed to the utmost; and sold by public auction if the tax be not paid; but the whole the business has been one tissue of infamous injustice from beginnii to end."—*Hon. F. J. Shore.*

Famines.

"Famines prevailed in India, in 1766, 1770 (when half the inhabitants perished in Bengal), 1782, 1792, 1803, 1804, 1819, 1820, 1824, 1829, 1832, 1833, 1836, 1837, and now in 1838, threatening the whole country, from Cutch to Cape Cormorin.

During the famine of 1837-38, the rivers were choked with dead bodies in the provinces where this very abundance of waste land existed; the air putrified with the stench of dead and dying human beings and animals; the jackals and vultures were seen preying on the still animated bodies of our fellow-creatures; mothers drowned their children by night, unwilling that the morning sun should witness their famishing state; and whole families of respectability poisoned themselves rather than beg a little rice for their support—although a rupee's worth (two shillings) of grain would sustain a man for thirty days! Hydrophobia was becoming as prevalent as cholera! and general mortality ensued.

"The deaths in Agra from famine in 1837-38, were at the rate of 10,000 a month, a destruction of life which would sweep off the whole population in less than a year."

Oriental Herald for February, 1839.

At Agra, the capital of the Emperor Akbar, which contained in his time 1,800,000 inhabitants,—at Agra, police officers were stationed along the banks of the river Jumna, to prevent mothers stealing down in the dead of night, and throwing their infants into the stream.

Export of rice from Calcutta (during the Agra famine of 1838) to Mauritius, to enable the people of that island to grow the sugar-cane, which the natives of India, who produce the rice, are prohibited from growing:—Bags, 230,371, of 164 pounds each, or 37,780,844 pounds. Rice exported to the French island of Bourbon during the same period, and for the same purpose, bags, 129,033, of 164 pounds each, or 21,161,412 pounds. Total export of rice from Calcutta in 1838, bags, 926,364, of 164 pounds each, or 151,923,696 pounds. Export of wheat, rice in the husk, beans, dholl, peas, flour, and bran, 163,362 Bazar maunds of 84 pounds each, or 13,722,408 pounds; facts shewing a power of surplus production so great, as to prove incontestibly that, although scarcity may occur, famine ought never to be known in any part of India.

Loss of revenue by the Agra famine, 1,000,420*l*., or 59 per cnt. of the whole amount of the taxes levied.

Opium Monopoly.

"In Benares, Behar, and throughout all the territories within the Company's jurisdiction, the cultivation of the poppy, the preparation of the drug, and the traffic in it, until it is brought to Calcutta and sold by auction for exportation, are under a strict monoply. Should an individual undertake the cultivation, without having 'entered into engagements with the government to deliver the produce at *the fixed rate*,' his property would be immediately attached, and the ryot compelled either to destroy his poppies, or give securities for the faithful delivery of the product. Nay, according to a late writer, '*the growing of opium is compulsory on the part of the ryot.*' Advances are made by Government through its native servants, and if a ryot refuses the advance, " the simple plan of throwing the rupees into his house is adopted; should he attempt to abscond, the peons seize him, tie the advance up in his clothes, and push him into his house. The business being now settled, and there being no remedy, he applies himself, as he may, to the fulfilment of his contract.'"—Taken from an article on the "Cultivation of the Poppy," in the *Chinese Repository* of February, 1837.

"The evils which the cultivation of opium entails upon our fellow-subjects in India, arise partly from the ryots in the opium districts of Patna and Benares being *compelled to give up fixed portions of their lands* for the production of the poppy.

"It is true that the Honorable Company pay fairly for the lands and labour thus wrested from the ryot* (farmer); and did the amount paid by the Government find its way honestly into the possession of these people, there might not be so much cause of complaint in this matter, but the contrary is the case. These payments have to pass through the hands of numerous *employés* of the Government; and scarce twenty per cent. of it ever reaches the legitimate owner.

"The evils of the cultivation, however, do not end here. In consequence of being obliged *forcibly* to cultivate this

---

* That is to say, they pay *their own price*, after the manner described in the preceding extract; a price so far below that at which it is exported, that, according to Mr. M'Culloch, the monopoly has sometimes produced a net revenue of *a million pounds sterling;* a sum, which, were free trade allowed, would be divided among the growers.

highly-taxed drug, the peasant is constantly exposed to a suspicion of retaining some part of the produce for private sale; the surveillance of the police is, therefore, especially directed to these unhappy creatures; and *the oppressions which they are subjected to in this way surpass belief.* They are exposed to every sort of annoyance which the ingenuity of the *authorized plunderers* (the police, and the custom-house searchers) can devise, in order to extort bribes."—"*Iniquities of the Opium Trade with China," by the Rev. A. S. Thelwall,* p. 162.

This is the manner in which the monopoly of opium is obtained in Bengal. It is then sold by the Company at quarterly sales; sold for export to China, where the drug is positively prohibited, and where the smuggling of it gives birth to scenes like the following, purposely acted before the eyes of the British residents. A man found guilty of keeping an opium smoking shop, was "brought to the quarter of Canton, separated for the use of the British and other foreigners, to be strangled in the square, in front of the factories."—*Canton Register* of the 13th of December, 1838.

In Bengal, the food-wanting ryot is obliged to produce opium for China. In China, the law-breaker is ignominiously executed for consuming it.

Abolition of Slavery, and the Slave Trade,

Attainable by the Encouragement of Free Labour in British India.

"Who in reality have been, though undesignedly, the greatest and foremost promoters of the slave trade? Who in the strictest truth, are still the most signal supporters, and encouragers of the traffic in human kind? Who are the persons, who, in point of fact, render hopeless and abortive every endeavour on the part of the governments of the world to put down this traffic, by creating such a temptation to employ slave labour in consequence of the price paid for its products, for its sugar, its cotton, its tobacco, its coffee, as to make the temptation irresistible to human cupidity? It is not attempted to be denied that the natives of India can produce sugar, cotton, tobacco, and coffee, *in the proportion that millions of men bear to hundreds.* It is admitted that they ask no more than to be suffered to produce these commodities; had they been so suffered fifty years ago, it is demonstrably certain that not a negro slave would now exist, *for he could not exist,* either in the West

Indies or America. In despite of every prohibition, the produce of slave labour at half a dollar a day, could not compete in any market with the produce of Indian labour at threepence a day. By the unerring operation of this simple gradual revolution had Providence designed and doomed the extinction of slavery throughout the civilized world. To whose account then, is justly and directly chargeable the amount of human woes with which this curse has filled and still fills the earth? Who have *proved* themselves to be the greatest foes to human advancement, and human happiness, the world has ever seen? Let those answer, whose measures have hitherto stultified every attempt to extend, on equitable principles, the cultivation of the produce of our possessions in the East."—*Extract from a Letter addressed to* ——— *by F. C. Brown, Esq., of Tellicherry.*

Answer to the Foregoing.

From the *Bombay Government Gazette*, 20 June, 1838.

"The Honorable the Court of Directors having been pleased TO DISAPPROVE of the notification of the 24th of February and 1st of August 1835, and of the 1st and 17th of November 1836, issued under the authority of Government by the Revenue Commissioners, *granting certain exemptions from assessment to lands cultivated with Cotton and the Mauritius' Sugar-cane*, AND TO DIRECT THAT SUCH NOTIFICATION BE IMMEDIATELY RECALLED; the Right Honorable the Governor in council is pleased hereby to CANCEL THE SAID NOTIFICATIONS *from this date.*"

Ruinous Effects of the Revenue System.

"Perhaps some of my Indian readers may recollect, in a village or country town in England, the excitement produced by the event of any poor man having his goods seized for rent; the sympathy universally felt for the sufferer, even though his own misconduct may have been the cause of his ruin; and the general indignation against the 'hard-hearted landlord.' Yet *here hundreds and thousands are fleeced of every thing*, while scarce an expression of pity is uttered by the English community. Young men in charge of the revenue talk with the utmost *sang froid* of attaching estates by hundreds with a view to their sale; and even the phrase, 'The district is almost ruined,' is constantly made use of without causing any feelings of abhorrence. It may certainly be said in excuse, that habit reconciles us to almost any thing. Does the sun of India dry up our sympathies; that in this country there is no one to stand forth as the poor man's friend? We may form some idea of the effect of our revenue system, in the valuation of lands ordered by Government, in suits for estates, with a view to rate the fees for stamps and lawyers. In the upper provinces *the land is to be valued at the rate of one year's rents;* where the permanent settlement exists, at three years; and in rent-free estates at eighteen years. What would be thought in England of a system of government which should reduce the value of land to *one year's purchase,* at which price even few purchasers were to be found?"—*Hon. F. J. Shore*, vol. i. p. 272.

"The whole system of our government has hitherto been, practically, that of *extortion and injustice to the people*, for the sake of partial and temporary profit; so that, while the country in general has enjoyed peace from all external aggression, ever since it was subjected to our authority, *its native inhabitants have become every year more impoverished.* The mode which we introduced of collecting the revenue, and the punishment awarded to the defaulters, will fully bear out this assertion.

In one year alone, *nearly one-tenth* of the whole land of Bengal, Behar, and Orissa, *was advertised for sale for revenue balances.* Surely such proceedings as these must have been chiefly caused by *excessive taxation and mis-government.*"—*Ibid*, vol. ii. 84.

"The summary is, that *the British Indian Government has been, practically, one of the most extortionate and oppressive that ever existed in India*, one under which injustice has been, and may be, committed, both by the government and by individuals, provided the latter be rich, to an almost unlimited extent, and under which *redress from injury is almost unattainable;* the consequence of which is, that *we are abhorred by the people, who would hail with joy, and instantly join, the standard of any power whom they thought strong enough to occasion our downfall.*"—*Ibid*, vol. ii. p. 521.

Sir Thomas Munro admitted, that in Malabar, for instance, there were 40,000 landholders, formerly tax free, now little above the rank of common cultivators, from whom we take 90 and sometimes 100 per cent. of the proprietor's rent, thereby annihilating one species of property, his rent as a landlord.

Major General Briggs says—"Under the present system it would be of no avail, even if the soil produced gold instead of grain, while the government take all the produce, except what is necessary to pay the labourers; there is no surplus to purchase manufactures; the country is absolutely without the means of even improving its soil."—*Briggs on the Land Tax of India*, p. 458.

The same officer says—"We treat the people as if they were savages."

Testimony of a Committee of the House of Commons.

A committee of the House of Commons some years ago declared—"*that the whole revenue system resolved itself, on the part of the public officers, into habitual extortion and injustice,*" whilst "what was left to the ryot (peasant) was little more than what he was enabled to procure by evasion and concealment."

"The land-tax of India (says Mr. Rickard), with the exactions of its rapacious collectors, is the very utmost the wretched inhabitants are able to pay. *Flesh and blood can yield no more.*"

Ryotwar System of Madras.

Evidence of the late James Mill, Esq., the organ of the East India Company, before the House of Commons.

3121. The rate fixed (on the land) was the maximum. Though this be fixed as the maximum that the ryot shall ever pay, it rarely happens he is able to pay so much; and that being the case, a sort of bargain is to be made with him annually to ascertain how much of the amount he can pay.

3321. According to the working of Sir F. Munro's ryotwar system, a species of settlement is to be made with the ryot annually; every year before harvest his crops are surveyed, in order to ascertain whether he will be able to pay the maximum for that year, or whether an abatement must be made, and to what extent.

In other words, the maximum is the fixed point, round which the collector and his native myrmidons are perpetually revolving, always trying to approach, but, being unattainable, never reaching.

Demoralizing Effects of British Rule.

"It is greatly to be deplored that in places the longest under our rule, there is the largest amount of depravity and crime. My travels in India have fallen little short of 8000 miles, and extended to nearly all the cities of importance in Northern, Western, and Central India. I have no hesitation in affirming that in the Hindoo and Mussulman cities, removed from European intercourse, there is much less depravity than either in Calcutta, Madras, or Bombay, where Europeans chiefly congregate."—*Captain Westmacott.*

"Mortifying as it may be to our vanity and self-love, it is notorious to all who mix with the people, and indeed, generally allowed by almost every Englishman in India, that the more the natives have been brought into contact with the English, the more has their character deteriorated. Immorality and crime have increased; and many vices adopted from which they were formerly free."—*The Hon. F. J. Shore.*

"The longer we have had the districts, the more apparently do lying and litigation prevail; the more are morals vitiated; the more are rights involved in doubt; the more are the foundations of society shaken; the more has the work of civil government become a hopeless, thankless toil; unsatisfactory as to its immediate results, hopeless as to its future effects."

The Right Hon. Holt Mackenzie.

From an Address delivered before the Relief Synod of Scotland, on the 14*th May* 1839, *by Mr. George Thompson.*

THE government and people of this country have a sacred, weighty, and imperative duty to perform to the Natives of India—a duty which can no longer be neglected without guilt, danger, bloodshed, and the ultimate loss of the fairest and richest portion of our distant possessions. In India there is a population of one hundred millions to be cared for. There is poverty to be relieved—misery to be succoured—famine to be averted—taxation to be lessened—disease to be cured—ignorance to be enlightened—slavery to be abolished—disaffection to be allayed—idolatry to be vanquished. The reign of righteousness must be substituted for the reign of terror and injustice. The wrongs of past ages must be redressed by the bestowment of enlightened and benign institutions, and the diffusion of the blessings which a country like this has in its power, and should feel it a privilege to confer. Our gross, and often ludicrous ignorance of Indian affairs, has long been matter of surprise and bitter contempt amongst the enlightened natives, and European residents of India. As a natural consequence of entire ignorance, there has been manifest an almost total indifference to the claims and welfare of the country. And yet there is, perhaps, no country in the world more replete with all that is calculated to fire the imagination, inflame the patriotism, and affect the hearts of the people of this nation. The student in history—the lover of antiquity—the admirer of stupendous monuments of industry and skill—the worshipper of the great and grand in nature—the political economist—the speculator in the rise and fall of empires—the friend of education—the patron of commerce—the promoter of missions—the emancipator of the slave:—all these may find, in the past history and present state of India, abundant food for reflection, and a boundless field for benevolent exertion. What has been our conduct, and what is our relation to India? We went there in the character of peaceful merchants, but we became warriors, conquerors, and finally princes. Upon the history of our acquisitions I will not dwell. If our path to supremacy were narrowly traced, I fear that every step would be found marked with blood. I believe there was too much truth in the saying of a great man, that India had been gained and kept by the power of the sword. We are, at the present moment, the rulers of a country as large as Europe, and of a people estimated at one hundred millions in numbers. From an investigation of the most authentic sources of information, it appears evident, that the connexion of India with Great Britain has not been productive of those benefits to the former which might have been anticipated. At this moment, there is in full operation a ruinous system of taxation. The mode of collecting the revenue is lable to every abuse, and to bribery, extortion, and frequently to cruelty of the most atrocious description. Odious monopolies exist. The treatment of the natives by European functionaries is a subject of universal discontent and complaint. Slavery exists in many parts of India, and of the very worst kind. There has been a culpable neglect of all the means of internal improvement and prosperity. The fiscal regulations of the country are of the most absurd and depressive character. The British Government has afforded its sanction to the idolatrous practices of the natives, and has polluted its treasury with the taxes wrung from the fainting pilgrims to the shrine of Juggernaut, and the banks of the Ganges.